FORBIDDEN
The Story of British Guiana

by

CHEDDI JAGAN

with a foreword
by
TOM DRIBERG, M.P

HANSIB PUBLISHING LIMITED
LONDON

First printed 1954

Reprinted January 1955

Reprinted in 1989 by Hansib Publishing Limited and included in the "Coolie Odyssey" series of books produced to mark the 150th anniversary of the abolition of slavery and the beginning of Indian Indenture in the Westindies.

Produced and printed in Britain by Hansib Publishing Limited, Tower House, 139/149 Fonthill Road, London N4 3HF. England.

ISBN 1 870518 23 3

The "Coolie odyssey" series:

India in the Caribbean

Benevolent Neutrality: Indian Government Policy and Labour Migration to British Guiana 1854-1884

The Web of Tradition: Uses of Allusion in V.S. Naipaul's Fiction

The Open Prison

The Second Shipwreck: A Study of Indo-Caribbean Literature

Indo-Westindian Cricket

Coolie Odyssey

Inseparable Humanity: An Anthology of Reflections by Shridath S. Ramphal

The King of Carnival and Other Stories

CONTENTS

PREFACE

by Cheddi Jagan, 1989

In 1953, the British ruling class, in the interests of the plantocracy of British Guiana, proclaimed the 'Lyttleton Doctrine' (Sir Oliver Lyttleton, linked to the Guinness monopoly, was Secretary of State for the Colonies). It sanctioned the use of military force to protect imperial interests: "Her Majesty's Government would not tolerate the establishment of communist states in the British Commonwealth".

This Doctrine, relating to the Commonwealth, was part and parcel of the Truman Doctrine which was worldwide in its applicability.

US President Harry Truman, at Baylor University on 6th March 1947, had made a speech on foreign policy which clearly stated that governments which had planned economies and controlled foreign trade were dangers to freedom – that freedom of speech and worship were dependent on the free enterprise system. He pointed out that controlled economies were "not the American way" and "not the way of peace". Truman urged that "the whole world should adopt the American system" and that "the American system could survive in America only if it became a world system". Calling for action, he implored: "Unless we act and act decisively, it [government-controlled economy and government-controlled foreign trade] will be the pattern of the next century ... if this trend is not reversed, the Government of the United States will be under pressure, sooner or later, to use these same devices to fight for markets and for raw materials".

Winston Churchill, who as Prime Minister despatched troops to British Guiana in 1953, had, as Leader of the Opposition in the House of Commons, issued the clarion call for the break-up of the anti-Hitler coalition and the start of the Cold War. He urged a western alliance against socialism and revolution which had its origins in the success of the Great October Socialist Revolution in the then Tsarist Russia. At that time he had called for a strangling of the "Bolshevik infant in its cradle". Later, although the Teheran Conference in November 1943 had reached agreement on a future post-war world to be built against fascism and on the foundation of Anglo-Soviet-American co-operation, Churchill was preoccupied with a "black depression" that, with the defeat of Hitler, the main task was to defeat "the bloody Russians". This was in line with the 1942 Memorandum which began the planning of the Cold War. It led to the deliberate delay in the opening of the World War II second front in France until June 1944, no doubt based on a hope that the Germans and Soviets would exhaust and destroy each other.[1]

At Westminster College in Fulton, Missouri, USA, on 5th March 1946 Churchill, in his "Iron Curtain" speech, referred to the "police governments" in Eastern Europe, warned of "Communist Fifth Columns" everywhere, which were a "growing challenge and peril to civilisation", and called for joint action in bringing about, through a preponderance of military power, "good understanding"; namely, a showdown with the USSR, the leaders of which he had always previously regarded as "murderers and ministers of hell".

The immediate aim was to shore up the tottering reactionary régime in Greece which was threatened by a popular partisan movement. The USA took control of the situation from the British and it was in order to rationalise their indefensible support for the return of the monarchy and the unpopular rightist government in Greece that the Truman Doctrine was outlined.[2]

The strategic objective was to "contain communism" and to arrest national and social liberation, and furthermore to make the US free enterprise capitalist system into a world system. A global strategy – military, political, economic, diplomatic and psychological – was accordingly devised.

An iron-ring of military bases was thus established under treaties covering different regions of the world: the International Treaty of Reciprocal Assistance (Rio Pact) for Latin America and the Caribbean; the North Atlantic Treaty Organisation (NATO) for the North Atlantic; the Baghdad Pact, later the Central Treaty Organisation (CENTO), for the Middle East; the Anzus Pact and South-East Asia Treaty Organisation (SEATO) for South-East Asia and the Pacific. The intention was not only to "contain communism", but also to rollback socialism worldwide.

Aid with strings was provided for Europe under the Marshall Plan (1947) and under Point Four and the Colombo Plan for Asia,

Africa, Latin America and the Caribbean. France, Italy and Belgium received US Marshall Aid on condition that communists and left-socialists were removed from the United Front governments which had been founded on the broad-based underground, anti-fascist resistance movements.

The Central Intelligence Agency (CIA) was established in 1948 for the purpose of overt and covert actions. In June 1953, the same year as that of the overthrow of the PPP government, the Mossadegh government of Iran was destabilised by the CIA. And a year later, the Arbenz government in Guatemala became a victim of CIA covert and indirect military action. **It is relevant to note, in view of the present-day solicitude of western leaders for democracy and human rights, that the three deposed governments had all been popularly elected at free and fair elections.** In fact, the PPP, though dubbed 'communist', won three consecutive elections in 1953, 1957 and 1961, and would have won a majority of seats at the 1964 elections if the electoral system had not been manipulated and changed.

What happened in British Guiana (now Guyana), Iran and Guatemala were not isolated events. They coincided with the period of intense McCarthyism inside the USA. Under Senator Joseph McCarthy's red-witch-hunting Committee on Un-American Activities, American patriots – politicians, administrators, journalists, scholars, writers and actors, including the learned black scholar Dr W.E.B. Dubois and the famous actor/singer Paul Robeson – were hounded and blacklisted. Dubois and Robeson were prevented from travelling abroad through the confiscation of their passports; Robeson was also prevented from earning a living by the denial of concert halls. Twelve communist leaders were indicted in 1948 and several were imprisoned for five years, not for committing any overt illegal acts, but simply for believing in and teaching the doctrine of Marxism-Leninism. Under the thought-control Smith Act, they were convicted of "conspiracy", that is an alleged agreement to teach and advocate the violent overthrow of the government.

Behind the anti-communist hysteria, direct and indirect aggression and reactionary violence lay naked self-interest – from the British-owned Booker Bros. sugar monopoly and the US-Canadian bauxite monopoly in British Guiana; from the British oil monopoly in Iran; from the US United Fruit Company which had monopolised the land, railways and ports of Guatemala. Mohammed Mossadegh had nationalised the Anglo-Iranian Oil Company after it had refused to agree to revise an archaic oil agreement so as to bring it into line with the then 50/50 profit-sharing arrangement in Venezuela.[3] President Col. Jacobo Arbenz had implemented a land reform programme which removed the stranglehold of the United Fruit Company from the Guatemalan economy and peasantry.

Later, in 1955, in keeping with its 'divide-and-rule' strategy, the Conservative British government engineered a split in the PPP and fostered racial and working-class divisions. By the early 1960s, to 'communism' were added racial problems as excuses for the destabilisation of the third PPP government by the CIA and British Intelligence (MI5).

The list of interventions in violation of international law is long. The most prominent include the British-French-Israeli attack on Egypt in 1956, the overthrow of the Juan Bosch government of the Dominican Republic in 1965, the Joao Goulart government of Brazil in 1964, the Allende government of Chile in 1973, the destabilisation of the Michael Manley government of Jamaica in 1980 and the invasion of Grenada in 1983.

The 30 years which separate the gunboat action against Guyana in 1953 and Grenada in 1983 had one thing in common – anti-communist hysteria: Guyana, at the start of the Cold War under the Churchill-Truman axis, and Grenada, under a reactivated Cold War by the Reagan administration. Under the Reagan Doctrine, the "evil empire" was to be rolled back and the "Marxist virus" in Grenada was to be exterminated. The 1983 invasion of Grenada was in line with the massive intervention – with over 40,000 troops – in the Dominican Republic in 1965, when the United States assumed the right under the Johnson Doctrine (President Lyndon Johnson) to intervene in any country "threatened by communism".

Though 'communism' was the scapegoat in Guyana and the Dominican Republic, it should be noted that many of the victims were not communists: Bosch (revolutionary-democrat); Mossadegh (nationalist); Goulart (revolutionary-democrat); Manley (social democrat). Indeed, Mossadegh was anti-communist. Manley, in the view of the bauxite-aluminium transnationals, had committed the cardinal sin of imposing (in 1974) a bauxite levy, which increased revenues by nearly 600 per cent.[4]

In the case of Fiji, the reactionaries, who had engineered a military coup, were opposed to change. The excuse was ethnic (Indian) domination. Actually, the overthrown Alliance government, a coalition of the Fiji Labour Party and the National Federation Party, stood, like the PPP government, for a progressive policy. In a victory speech, Prime Minister Dr Timoci Bavadra, an ethnic Fijian, had promised "to ensure that the fruits of development are shared more fully". His cabinet, with an Indian majority, wanted to pursue a non-aligned and, like some other Pacific states, a non-nuclear policy. Palau Vanuatu, the Solomon Islands and New Zealand had declared themselves "nuclear-free" and decided not to permit the development of any US military facilities in the event of the closure of the US bases in the Philippines, nor to allow entry to any warship unless there was a guarantee that the ship was not nuclear-powered or nuclear-armed. These progressive policies were opposed by the conservatives. They saw Bavadra's election, as the *Sydney Morning Herald* put it, as "the end of an era of comfortable Anglophone politics".

The imperialists will use any convenient excuse to realise their aims. As former Canadian Prime Minister Pierre Trudeau, in relation to US aggression against Grenada, put it, the Americans "went into Grenada just to set up a different type of government".

About two decades earlier the US and British governments had resorted to what the then British Leader of the Opposition, Harold Wilson, called "a fiddled constitutional arrangement" – a changed voting system – to remove the third popularly-elected PPP government and install in power L.F.S. Burnham. This was the same Burnham about whom former US presidential adviser Arthur M. Schlesinger Jr., in his book *A Thousand Days: John F. Kennedy in the White House*, had written:

> " Thus far [May 1962] our policies had been based on the assumption that Forbes Burnham was, as the British described him, an opportunist, racist and demagogue intent only on personal power."

This description was somewhat similar to President F.D. Roosevelt's description of Nicaraguan dictator Somoza – "he is a son-of-a-bitch, but he is our son-of-a-bitch".

Guyana, more than two decades after independence, is a good example of what is in store for Grenada under a puppet régime. Its economy is a shambles. Indeed, it has become what the Jamaican sociology professor at Harvard University, Dr Orlando Patterson, called "a complete and total disaster".

The first pro-big business G$300-million six-year (1966-72) Development Plan, heavily weighted towards infrastructure, collapsed at the end of 1969. It had been formulated by economist Sir Arthur Lewis, who had earlier introduced into the Caribbean region the Puerto Rican model of development based on "industrialisation by invitation", and was implemented with the help of an Economic Adviser, W. Davenport (American) and the Governor of the Bank of Guyana, Horst Bockleman (West German).

Commenting on the grave situation, a one-time Economic Adviser to the Guyana government, Dr Wilfred David, disclosed just prior to his sudden departure in early 1971: "We have had growth without development. The problem has been exemplified by the high level of unemployment and foreign dependency".

By 1973 the economy was facing a crisis. This was averted by a windfall of over G$500 million from a levy on exports of sugar at astronomically high world prices. However, the end of 1976 saw the worst crisis ever. And despite lavish help from the US government and infusions from the International Monetary Fund (IMF), the then Vice-President in charge of Economic Planning and Finance, Desmond Hoyte, told the National Assembly: "To put it bluntly, the performance of the economy in 1981 was disastrous". On 14th February 1982, the *New Nation*, organ of the ruling People's National Congress (PNC), stated that the economy was"tottering on the brink of collapse".

The bankrupt situation was openly admitted by leading spokesmen of the ruling party and government. The then Vice-President and ruling PNC Chairman, Cammie Ramsaroop, said that "the nation is in the red". Desmond Hoyte, in his 1982 Budget Speech, pointed out:

> "In consequence, many suppliers have stopped exporting goods to us other than on a cash basis; and in some countries their export insurance agencies have withdrawn cover from us. We

are not deemed to be credit-worthy at this time."

The Minister of Finance stated that "the total national savings stands at zero ... Guyana has reached the stage where neither our debt at home nor abroad can be paid".

As an admission of failure and hopelessness, Minister of Finance Carl Greenidge, in his 1984 budget statement, said: "The production sector of Guyana has undergone a marked decline over the last three years". He further admitted that the picture of the economy, the strategies which were being recommended and the prognoses for speedy resuscitation "all appear very daunting", and concluded that he could "offer no comforting solution which will allow us to survive and prosper".

In 1985, Guyana was declared by the IMF to be "ineligible" for further credits – a distinction shared by only two other countries!

In an understatement contained in his 1987 budget speech, the Finance Minister said:

> "Economic growth since 1980 has been very sluggish. In fact, since the turn of the decade, apart from the last three years, the economy has experienced negative economic growth. But, with the exception of 1984, that growth has been relatively small."

Actually, there had been a drastic decline: minus 10.8 per cent in 1982; minus 9.9 per cent in 1983; 2.2 per cent in 1984; 1.0 per cent in 1985; 0.3 per cent in 1986; 0.7 per cent in 1987; minus 3 per cent in 1988.

Early in 1987, under IMF pressure, the Guyana dollar was devalued by 127 per cent at the Guyana Central Bank rate and 388 per cent at the commercial banks' "open window" rate. It was claimed that this would stimulate industrial and agricultural development, stop illegal foreign exchange dealings in Georgetown's so-called "Wall Street" and curb the parallel market. But the latter has grown whilst the economic growth rate in 1987 and 1988 was far below the projected 3%. Production in the three main sectors of the economy – sugar, bauxite and rice – was far below the levels reached in 1964, the last year of the PPP government.

The calamitous situation has resulted in a per capita Gross Domestic Product (GDP) of US$410, the lowest of the 13 Caricom states, and among the three lowest in Latin America and the

Caribbean (the other two being Bolivia and Haiti). At the time of the PPP government in the early 1960s, Guyana was bracketed with the more developed countries (MDCs) – Jamaica, Barbados and Trinidad and Tobago.

Other economic indicators show a far worse situation in the "lost decade" (1975-1985), as compared with other Third World countries, especially in the context of our vast natural resources. The most alarming is the huge and chronic budget deficit. On this score, the Minister of Finance, in his budget speech of 1986, told the National Assembly that most of the foreign financial institutions like the World Bank, the Inter-American Development Bank (IDB) the European Investment Bank (EIB) and the European Development Fund (EDF) "seem to be increasingly pre-occupied with the size of our fiscal deficit". Yet, the deficit is growing.

Two factors are mainly responsible for the financial crisis: an overbloated military and bureaucratic apparatus and excessive debt payments.

The huge debt has become a burden on the backs of the people. The debt service ratio (external debt payments in relation to export income) was nearly 30% in 1988, far too high. In 1988, the Guyana government decided to pay US$112 million with the expectation of net external borrowing of US$27 million.

What is being paid out is sorely needed for the importation of consumer necessities as well as spare parts and machinery to turn the wheels of industry. Since 1979, when the government breached a minimum wage agreement, the spineless PNC regime has consistently refused to heed our advice to suspend debt payments or pay only a portion, or to follow the example of Peru and Zambia and limit external debt payments to 10% of foreign earnings.

Debt payments have led to the shortage of foreign exchange and the big import cuts. The consequent shortages are affecting not only production and productivity but also people's livelihood. In the colonial era a 1942 cost of living survey in the capital, Georgetown, disclosed that a worker earned $7.41 but spent $8.23 per week. In the present period of neo-colonialism, the position is worse. A family budget survey conducted by the Economic and Research Committee of the Trade Union Congress (TUC) disclosed that in 1981 the expenses of a worker's family of six were G$654 but his income was only G$250 per month. This caused TUC General

Secretary Joseph Pollydore to comment that life had become unbearable for the worker: "he was eating one meal a day and his child was going to school with bare tea in the morning". Since then the quality of life has sharply deteriorated.

In 1964 goods were plentiful and the PPP government paid part of the price on essential commodities as a subsidy. There was also strict price control. Now, there are shortages, hardly any subsidies and practically no price controls.

Social services and social infrastructure have also deteriorated. The percentage budget allocation for this sector has declined by about half compared with 1964. Security gets a bigger allocation than health, housing, co-operatives and transport combined.

There is a marked lowering of the standards of education. Guyana takes last place in the English-speaking Caribbean in external examination results and is well on its way to becoming a nation of "functional illiterates". In the mid-1970s a former Minister of Education had stated that three-quarters of the children coming out of primary school could not read properly. Since then the position has worsened.

Health services have declined. The disgraceful practice of "two-patients-in-one-bed" (a small bed for one person), even in maternity cases, continues. And the scourge of malaria, which had been virtually eradicated by the PPP government, is raising its ugly head alarmingly.

The housing problem is acute, and rapidly deteriorating living standards alongside conditions of high unemployment and under-employment have led to an exacerbation of anti-social acts. Crime has reached alarming proportions. Choke-and-rob has been superceded by armed gangs. Criminals with weapons invade homes and business places, not only committing robberies, but also murdering their victims.

The Hoyte administration is placing its hopes on a new IMF agreement and foreign investment. It is looking for US$600 million over the next three years. And visits have been made to the centres of world capitalism to woo investors.

To secure IMF credits and loans from the World Bank and Western governments the PNC government is being forced to make concessions – political, economic, institutional, ideological – as required by Washington. The US perception of Guyana was set out by the Santa Fe Committee, a group of hawkish advisers to President Reagan, whose 1980 report, "A New Inter-American Policy for the Eighties", saw changes in the Caribbean as being the result of some "Moscow intrigues".

The Burnham administration, with IMF agreement, had in 1978 (after the nationalisation of the sugar and bauxite companies in the 1974-76 period) reverted from a firm domestic and foreign anti-imperialist position to a policy of vacillation, as in the 1971-73 period, with an unmistakeable bias towards imperialism.

That somersault, however, did not help. By 1982 the country and people were in a worse state. It was in that year that Burnham dubbed the new IMF proposals for a steep devaluation and additional pressures on the working people, as a "recipe to riot" and called for modified terms from the international body.

Now, step by step, the new administration is retreating. The PNC has placed itself in this undesirable position as a result of its policies and actions over the years. Lack of democracy, racial and political discrimination, favouritism, nepotism, extravagance and corruption have fettered the productive forces, inhibited production and productivity and put the nation in a debt trap.

Having rejected the call of the PPP for a political solution and the formation of a National Patriotric Front Government, the PNC regime is genuflecting before imperialism and the transnational corporations. To secure aid (loans and grants), the country is being forced to submit to the "conditionality" of the imperialist-controlled IMF and World Bank and the Caribbean Basin Initiative (CBI).

The CBI was proposed as an economic aid package for "those countries which are under economic siege". It is basically the economic aspect of an anti-communist and militarist strategy for the Caribbean.

Before a country is allowed to join the CBI club (Cuba, Nicaragua and Grenada under Maurice Bishop were excluded), and thus qualify for loans and duty-free entry of certain goods into the USA, it must meet certain requirements. The United States "will discuss with each of these countries their own measures of self-help".

This means the imposition of political strings – "create conditions under which ... private entrepreneurship and self-help can flourish"; create an investment climate for foreign capital with income tax holidays, subsidised services, etc; guarantees against expropriation; if properties are nationalised, the payment of "prompt, adequate and effective compensation"; unrestrained repatriation of profits and other assets; no limitation on the "freedom of trade".

The Guyana government's pronouncements on privatisation and nationalisation and its "open door" policy to foreign private capital are in accord with this "conditionality" and are a complete reversal of the positive aspects of the Sofia Declaration of December 1974, which stated that natural and national resources and foreign trade would come under the control of the state and that foreign capital would be welcomed but only in partnership with the state and/or co-operatives. They are also a retreat from the New Investment Code of 1979, which reserved for the state the strategic sectors of the economy.

Today, in the context of a looming recession and a trade war, the prospects for the development of Guyana with the main reliance placed on foreign private capital are remote. Many countries in Latin America – Mexico, Brazil, Argentina, Chile – which carried out a policy of modernisation with foreign capital under a system of dependent capitalism are in serious trouble. The South-East Asian societies – Singapore, Taiwan, south Korea and Hong Kong – which were held out as models for Third World countries are also facing problems.

Their modernisation was based on the premise that the foreign investors had the capital, the know-how (technology) and the markets. Now they are told that they must balance their trade with the USA. According to the United Nations about 50 per cent of Latin American commodities face restrictions to their entry into the USA, the European Community and Japan. Several dozen Brazilian commodities were banned from entry by the US government in early 1988.

Experience shows that the transnational corporations chose the labour-intensive and "dirty" industries for the Third World countries. Now, faced with protectionism and tariff and non-tariff barriers, they are pursuing the big countries like India and China which have a huge internal market.

Guyana has neither the basic infrastructure – water, gas, electricity, telephone, transport – for industries, nor a sufficiency of technologically-skilled and semi-skilled workers. The major interest so far shown by foreign investors is in the extraction of gold and oil (petroleum).

Gold is a wasting asset and the country does not derive the benefit from much that is mined. And petroleum extraction alone, though important, is not a panacea for Third World countries' ills as Trinidad and Tobago, Nigeria, Venezuela, Mexico and other oil-producers have demonstrated.

Our country was also to become the graveyard for industrial waste from the USA and elsewhere – waste which cannot be disposed of in its countries of origin. To the existing economic and social crises the minority PNC regime was preparing the way for an ecological crisis. Our environment was under threat. What an alarming picture: digging out from our soil precious metals and minerals and depositing therein poisonous waste! What Caricom countries had rejected, Guyana, on the road to betrayal, was accepting. To the tragedies of Jim Jones 'Jonestown' and thallium sulphide poisoning, the regime was preparing the way for others. Fortunately, strong internal opposition and regional pressures forced the government to abandon the project.

Apart from the economic concessions, which also include partial privatisation of state enterprises, there is also political accommodation. For example, the government admitted that it had changed its position on a United Nations resolution on Kampuchea: from a negative vote in 1985 to an abstention in 1986.

Moreover a red carpet welcome was extended to the Grenadian Governor-General, Sir Paul Schoon, who had issued the 'invitation' to the invading Americans. This no doubt was intended to please the US government.

Schoon's visit was also in line with the Hoyte government's application to the USA to join the CBI, in other words to fall in line with the strategic plans of imperialism to control the Caribbean region politically, economically, militarily and culturally.

These are clear indications of an accommodation with imperialist interests. Little wonder, then, that World Bank Vice-President for Latin America and the Caribbean, David Knox, said: "We see good prospects now of being able to help the Guyanese government to work (out) the kind of programme which would obtain financial support from donors".[5] And the US Private Investment Corporation (OPIC),once again after the lapse of a decade, started giving insurance to companies wishing to invest in Guyana.[6]

However, the economic and social crisis will not be solved without a solution to the political crisis, leading to full democracy and the meaningful involvement of the people at all levels. It is to be noted that, despite generous assistance by the IMF, World Bank and US and other Western governments, the economy was in a worse state than when the first IMF agreement was signed in mid-1978. The marked deterioration was noted by the report (October 1982) of the IMF:

> "Economic activity in Guyana has been depressed for the last several years. During the 1977-81 period, real GDP (Gross Domestic Product) declined by close to nine per cent and the rate of inflation increased from less than 10 per cent in 1977 to 29 per cent in 1981."

In 1976, at the time of the imperialist counter-offensive following the nationalisation of the sugar and bauxite industries, the PPP had warned that, if our 17-point programme was not implemented, Guyana would later find itself in an economic crisis, following which, in the search for foreign aid, the anti-imperialist gains made in the 1975-76 period would be sacrificed. This is precisely what is taking place today.

And the resultant discontent and alienation are leading to a human resource crisis. In July 1967, a PNC supporter writing in the *Sunday Graphic* under the pen-name of Lucian pointed out:

> "Many Guyanese and non-Guyanese are disgusted with the present state of affairs in this country. Some are packing up to leave out of sheer frustration, while others are dejected from unbearable disgust."

Today, the trickle of two decades ago has turned into a flood of the able-bodied, skilled, semi-skilled and white collar workers and professionals.

The corrupt society which has been created by the PNC, under the system of bureaucratic-state, parasitic and co-operative capitalism, has been fully documented in the Report by the Integrity Commission. It is a serious indictment of the PNC, which has brought our nation to economic, social and, now confirmed, moral ruin. It fully justifies the position taken by the PPP for over two decades.

The Report referred to "a get-rich-quick syndrome" and "bribery and corruption ... which ... has reached if not, then almost, epidemic proportions", and noted that a "number of public officers seem to think that public funds are there for the taking". Hitting out against racial and political discrimination, the Commission observed that "selection and promotion on merit are sacrificed on the altar of political partisanship, party loyalty, nepotism and personal friendship". As regards sexual harassment, the Report stated: "We have formed the impression from the evidence generally, that, as regards sexual gratification, public office holders show particular favour to those who submit to their urge to be sexually gratified."

In its concluding remarks, it noted:

> "Guyana needs a new moral vitality. A fresh flow of values must now be infused into the life-stream of society, revitalising its sinews. Indiscipline, inattention, discourtesy, all symptoms of malaise, of inertia, fraud and other corrupt, immoral and dishonest acts – the cumulative effect of all these social ills, which are so manifest in the public sector bodies, seriously hinders progress."

As to the Commissioners' observation about the need for electoral reforms and their recommendation that "the government and all the political parties concerned hold urgent and constructive discussions with a view to agreeing on other provisions for further reforms to be made to the electoral laws", the government spokesmen were at pains to point out that the question of electoral reforms was outside their terms of reference.

This is ridiculous as electoral fraud in all elections since 1968 and in the referendum of 1978 is the foundation of many corrupt practices. The Commissioners, noting the interconnection and interplay between electoral fraud and corruption generally, were duty-bound to recognise the need and call for electoral reforms. As they correctly put it, the government must set the example, the moral tone, if corruption is to be stamped out.

INTERDEPENDENCE

The late Guyanese journalist, Carl Blackman, in October 1987, noted: "...sometimes I feel that if there had been no suspension [of the Constitution in 1953] we would be a happier, prosperous nation today".

This was exactly the point I had made in California in 1974 in a conversation at the Rand corporation, a think-tank of the US State Department. My son's graduation from the University of California had facilitated a US visa. For the previous ten years, I was denied one, although I held the official position of Leader of the Opposition!

Referring to the CIA's covert acts of destabilisation in Guyana in the early 1960s, I said that the same Cold War policy had led ultimately to a fiasco in Vietnam, to the radicalisation of the American people and an economic debacle – recession, a trade deficit, devaluation of the "almighty" (good-as-gold) dollar and non convertibility of the dollar into gold. I cited statistics indicating a decline in production in Guyana in the seven year period (1965-72) as compared with the seven year period (1957-64) of the PPP government. Referring to the 30 per cent cut in Guyana's imports in 1973/74, and generalising this to other Third World countries, I asked: how does putting people like Burnham in power help to stimulate world trade and the getting of jobs for people in the United States? At that time of recession, American industry was operating at around 60-65 per cent capacity.

Pointing out that, as a student of history, I saw US actions in Guyana as part of a process unleashed with the Cold War, I added that I had no feelings of recrimination. However, the crisis in the North, I said, would not be solved by rearing client states like Guyana. **Strange as it might sound, I said that it was not politicians like Burnham, but rather like me, who should be supported in the Third World. Only we have the support and confidence of the people, and without that there can be no development. But we were not asking for support; all we wanted was a "hands off" policy.**

A second encounter with the Americans came at a conference in the Venezuelan capital, Caracas, in 1983 on the occasion of the Bicentennial of Simon Bolivar. At a session on US – Latin

American relations, I posed the question: What did the United States want – a huge and costly armament programme and abandonment of the "war on poverty" at home, coupled with domination and plunder[7] of Latin American and Caribbean countries or a "good neighbour" policy of mutual respect, live-and-let-live and genuine interdependence? IMF prescriptions, I pointed out, had led to underdevelopment, increased unemployment, poverty and hunger. When the people fought back, as in El Salvador, they were terrorised, tortured and killed by the dictators and their death squads, who were propped up by US bayonets and dollars. How could the US economy become viable when Latin American and Caribbean countries were forced to curtail essential imports (needed for their own development) so as to have a foreign exchange surplus for the payment of debts, which by 1982 accounted for some 59 per cent of foreign earnings? What was needed was a new policy for recovery of both the North and the South, in keeping with the Brandt Commission's thesis of interdependence and mutual development.

More recently, in February 1988, I took part in a US Congressional Consultation on the Caribbean Basin Initiative (CBI) in Barbados. Not only were there generalised criticisms of this programme; also voiced were attacks on the US administration for quota cuts of Caribbean sugar exports and for cutbacks in US aid.

Congressman Dante D. Faschell, Chairman of the US House of Representatives Committee on Foreign Affairs, though expressing sympathy and support for the Caribbean, pleaded for realism and an appreciation, also, of the problems facing the United States - a huge federal budget deficit, sustained calls for welfare, the need to protect jobs and a large number of sugar workers in his own constituency in Florida.

In my contribution, I expressed agreement with Congressman Faschell that we must take a comprehensive approach, keeping in mind both the interests of the United States and the Caribbean. I pointed out, however, that if the Consultation was kept within the narrow confines of the CBI, then our efforts would be fruitless, and the CBI would fail like the Alliance for Progress[8]. If the CBI were to succeed, first of all its Cold War underpinnings must be removed: the Reagan/Gorbachov talks had created a favourable international atmosphere for such a development. Moreover, I pointed out, if the basic needs of the United States and Caribbean peoples were to be met, and an explosion in the Caribbean, as in the late 1930s, was to be averted, it was necessary to:

1. Support the United Nations call for 'disarmament for development';
2. Agree to a 12 per cent cut in defence expenditure by the nuclear powers, with the proceeds to be used to pay the transnational banks for the cancellation of repayments on loans to Third World countries;
3. Agree to hold, under UN auspices, a "global round" of discussions for a New International Economic Order to institute more equitable economic relations between the North and the South;
4. Support democratisation worldwide.

I was pleased to see that some of the ideas I expressed were later voiced by the Rev. Jesse Jackson, especially in his presentation of a budget for the USA. In the Democratic primaries he proposed increased welfare at the expense of the defence budget. No doubt that was one of the reasons why he was also attracting white voters. His advocacy was universal and his message, directed to the poor, unemployed and homeless, crossed racial barriers.

This lesson has to be learnt the hard way; **if there is to be world recovery, the Burnhams/Hoytes, the Pinochets and the Gairys/Blaizes of this world, installed and propped up by imperialism, cannot help to bring it about.**

Guyana was once regarded as the greatest asset and hope for the Commonwealth Caribbean territories. But this potential was not fulfilled. In 1975, university lecturer, Dr John Dukhia, in a report presented to the 10th West Indies Agricultural Economic Conference, pointed out that Guyana had the lowest consumption of meat per person in the more developed Caricom countries. "This," he commented, "is rather paradoxical since it is generally argued that Guyana has the potential of being the food basket of the Caribbean."

Today, instead of being the food basket, Guyana is regarded as a basket case; it is a liability to its Caricom partners. It is highly indebted to Trinidad and Tobago and Barbados. Its indebtedness has caused the collapse of the Caribbean Multilateral Clearing Facility.

The prospects under the ruling People's National Congress are bleak. The TUC Economic and Research Committee in its 1986 Report noted that "it is difficult to foresee any significant improvement in Guyana's economy". It is only the Maurice Bishops, the Salvador Allendes and the Fidel Castros and others, supported by the people, who can increase production and stimulate world trade. This is realism.

Jingoism, anti-communist hysteria and Cold War confrontation and intervention must give way to respect for national independence and self-determination, detente, peaceful co-existence and peaceful competition. Otherwise, we will all burn. As Prime Minister Margaret Thatcher rightly said at the time of the Grenada invasion, if the United States decided to take over every country where "communism ruled", it would lead to "really terrible wars in the world".

The Cold War must be ended not only between West and East, the USA and USSR, but also between North and South, the developed capitalist states and the underdeveloped Third World countries.

The US administration's insistence on the observance of human rights must be translated into support for the Guyanese people for:

1. the holding of long overdue local government elections (last held and rigged in 1970) under an independent Elections Commission;
2. electoral reforms embracing –
   a) an independent chair of the Election Commission and Chief Elections Officer,
   b) restoration of the powers of the Elections Commission;
   c) the counting of the ballots at the place of poll;
3. Invitations to the Non-Aligned Movement Secretariat, the UN Commission on Human Rights, the Organisation of American States (OAS) Commission on Human Rights, the Caribbean Human Rights Internet and friendly governments to observe the next general elections.

The PPP, as in 1953, is continuing the struggle for working-class and racial unity. At the same time, it is committed to an alliance of all left and democratic forces. It has declared itself in favour of "winner-does-not-take-all" politics; namely, it would form a coalition government, even if it alone won a majority in a free and fair election. Only such a broad-based revolutionary-democratic government, necessary for economic, racial/cultural and security considerations, can get Guyana moving forward again.

The people's forces struggling for democracy and bread are growing. The tempo of consolidation has been quickening, particularly since 1978 and the anti-labour IMF agreement, when the PNC was forced for the first time to attack its own section of the working class. Unity is developing at the level of political parties, trades unions, farmers' organisations, middle strata, the radical intelligentsia, patriotic businessmen and the Church. These forces are now banding themselves around the Patriotic Coalition for Democracy (PCD).

The PCD is committed to struggle for the restoration of the fundamental rights laid down in the Guyana Constitution and the United Nations Covenant on Civil and Political Rights.

Developments regionally and internationally also favour the Guyanese people's struggle. There has been universal condemnation of electoral fraud in Guyana.

In the Third World the process of democratisation is gaining ground, the most recent manifestations being the downfall of military dictators in Argentina, Uruguay and Brazil, Marcos in the Philippines and "Baby Doc" Duvalier in Haiti. And the Gorbachov/ Reagan talks have opened new prospects for disarmament, world peace, detente and peaceful coexistence. As during World War II, with the anti-Hitler coalition, so today's world cries out for an anti-poverty, human welfare coalition, a world wide effort for a "war against poverty".

With the recent 150th Anniversary of the ending of Apprenticeship of slavery and the entry of Indo-Guyanese into Guyana, the struggle for national and social liberation is gaining strength. Let us, in paying tribute to our Afro- and Indo-Guyanese ancestors, who watered the sugar cane fields with their blood, sweat and tears, pledge to work for racial and working people's unity and to build a new Guyana with security for all, in keeping with our motto: one people, one nation, one destiny.

REFERENCES AND NOTES

1. In the USA also there were many isolationists who shared similar views. Senator Robert A. Taft had declared: "A victory for communism would be far more dangerous to the United States than a victory for fascism".

2. According to Roberto Gonsalez Gomes, "Isolationalism or Neo-Interventionism", Tricontinental 90, OSPAAL, Havana, 1974, p.5: "Worth recalling is the message sent by Ernest Bevin to the US government, expressing England's inability to intervene in the Greek civil war and to give military and economic aid to Turkey, which led to the proclamation of the so-called Truman Doctrine in March 1947 and the start of the "cold war".

"Winston Churchill is quoted in The New York Times, April 12, 1947: "'On Greek affairs in 1944-45 I seemed to find myself out of step. But today it seems I was pursuing the exact policy which, little more than two years later, the United States has adopted with strong conviction. This is to me a very intense satisfaction.'"

3. A group of US oil companies broke the British monopoly on Iran's oil, with a 40 per cent share in a new consortium of Western oil companies. According to David Wise and Thomas B. Ross, in their The Invisible Government, "General Fazollah Zahedi, the man the CIA chose to replace Mossadegh ... fought the Bolsheviks, was captured by the Kurds, and, in 1942, was kidnapped by the British, who suspected him of Nazi intrigues. During World War II the British and the Russians jointly occupied Iran. British agents, after snatching Zahedi, claimed they found the following items in his bedroom: "a collection of German automatic weapons, silk underwear, some opium, letters from German parachutists operating in the hills, and an illustrated register of Teheran's most exquisite prostitutes"."

4. Prof. Dr Norman Girvan had pointed out in a study that the Caribbean supplied about 86 per cent of the raw material requirement of the North American aluminium industry, but received only about four per cent of the net income of the vertically-integrated industry.

5. Sunday Chronicle, 3 January, 1988, p12.

6. Ibid.

7. According to the UN Commission for Latin America and the Caribbean, the net annual outflow from the region, in the form of *profits, principal and interest, in the 1981-85 period was US$36,000 million.*

8. About the reformist Alliance for Progress, Dante D. Faschell stated in 1969: "I would be less than frank if I would not admit that the initial record of the Alliance for Progress inspires more gloom than satisfaction."

FOREWORD

by TOM DRIBERG, M.P.

"Colonialism" is doubly a word of doom. It means hunger; and it means alien rule.

It is a word that ought to be obsolete by now. High sounding declarations of human rights have been subscribed to by all civilised nations; and successive British Governments, in that vein of moral earnestness which sceptical foreigners and ungrateful subject peoples unaccountably mistake for cant, have reaffirmed their desire speedily to assist those subject peoples "towards the goal of self-government".

The late Father Stanton used to tell of an old ex-convict who joined lustily in the hymns at mission services, especially in one whose refrain ended "Yes, I will follow thee to the goal"—only, unfortunately, he always misread the last word and bellowed "gaol".

The goal of self-government has turned out to be gaol indeed for Dr. Cheddi Jagan, the author of this book, who is, as I write this foreword, in prison in the land of which he was recently Prime Minister. His chief offence seems to have been that, unlike some politicians, he and his colleagues actually tried to carry out their election promises. This process included the introduction of reforms no more "left-wing" than the Beveridge Report or the Wagner Act; but the reforms alarmed the Americans and would have inconvenienced the London financiers who dominate the life of British Guiana and exploit its people; so the troops were sent, the Constitution suspended, and a "red plot" rigged up.

The London headlines accepted uncritically the Government propaganda story, but when the correspondents got to British Guiana they had to cable home, disappointingly, that there were no disturbances and no signs of any crisis. Nor, in Parliament, was Mr. Lyttelton able to justify the gravest of his charges, that of intended arson. This charge in particular had been played up in the sensational newspapers: naturally, they were less interested in reporting that the Government had run away from it in the House of Commons.

Never, surely, was such drastic action based on such vague hypotheses: "if" it had not been taken, claimed Mr. Lyttelton, a Communist state "might" have been set up in British Guiana. There is no "if" about the dictatorship of the Right now set up by the British Government. It is a strange way of teaching a subject people democracy: go ahead, vote freely—but if we don't like the results of your voting, we shall wash the whole thing out.

The Labour Party, in office, had at least shown the sincerity of its anti-imperialism by its actions in India and Burma and the Gold Coast. Its condemnation of Mr. Lyttelton's action in British Guiana was qualified and cautious; its leaders were uneasy because Dr. Jagan was known to have Communist associations. Perhaps all of us in the Labour Party have been to blame for not showing a more constant and active interest in all the colonial territories, including British Guiana: if we had done so, some of the emerging political leaders in those territories might not, in their despair, have turned elsewhere for comradeship and support.

I cannot myself endorse every word of Cheddi Jagan's book; but I met him more than once in London and learned to respect and like him for his obvious sincerity, his modesty, and his quiet, unembittered wit. It is, of course an *ex parte* book. How should it not be? The British people, fed with the sophistries and distortions of the White Paper, have a right to study the other side.

Relations between the "advanced" and the "backward" peoples are the most important problems in the world today. This book is the case-history of a classic example of *How Not To Do It.*

CHAPTER ONE

TOO FANTASTIC

"They respect the right of all peoples to choose the form of government under which they will live; and they wish to see sovereign rights and self-government restored to those who have been forcibly deprived of them."

THE ATLANTIC CHARTER

October 4, 1953, was a bright, sunny day. It was a Sunday—a day when one likes to read the newspapers in bed. But this day was different. There was an early knock at the door.

A friend shouted: "Have you heard the news? British soldiers are coming here. There's a rumour that the Constitution is to be suspended."

The news did not greatly disturb me. I thought the whole story was too fantastic. But during that day there was a great deal of excitement all over the capital. Georgetown was keyed up with the rumour. People were talking about it everywhere. I dismissed the whole affair as rumour-mongering. I told my associates there was no reason for all the excitement.

After all, who ever heard of the suspension of a Constitution in these days of freedom and the Universal Declaration of Human Rights?

But the rumour became a reality. For on Tuesday the first B.B.C. broadcast gave us the news. The British Government had issued a statement through the Colonial Office which said:

> "It has been evident that the intrigues of Communists and their associates, some in Ministerial posts, threaten the welfare and good administration of the colony. If these processes were to continue unchecked an attempt might be made by methods which are familiar in some others parts of the world to set up a Communist-dominated state. This would lead to bloodshed.
>
> "In view of the latest developments, Her Majesty's Government have felt it necessary to send naval and military forces to Georgetown (capital of British Guiana) with

the utmost despatch, in order to preserve peace, and the safety of all classes. Any reinforcements that may be necessary will be sent from the United Kingdom."

The cruiser *Superb* and the frigates *Bigbury Bay* and *Burghead Bay* were steaming from Bermuda. Troops were being flown from Jamaica. The aircraft carrier *Implacable* was to bring further reinforcements from the United Kingdom towards the end of the week.

The House of Assembly was in session during this crisis week. On Wednesday I moved the suspension of standing rules and orders to take a motion protesting against the despatch of British troops to British Guiana.

But the Speaker was in good form. He objected. He was "not aware" that troops had been despatched. Did he not hear the B.B.C. announcement, we asked. Did he not hear that troops were within territorial waters? Yes, but that was not evidence enough. He would allow the motion as soon as he was aware of their presence.

At 2 p.m. on the next day I again moved the suspension of standing orders to protest against the landing of troops. But the Speaker was still making the same gambit. He was not aware of the landing of troops. Had he seen them? Yes, but he was not officially informed. Who should inform him? His boss, the Governor, Sir Alfred Savage, who had appointed him. He would take the motion the next day. But, of course, there was no next day for this motion. For on the next day there was no House of Assembly.

On that day, October 9, ears were glued to radio sets. The Chief Secretary read in his inimitable, dry, emotionless, civil servant tones, the Statement of Her Majesty's Government:

> "Her Majesty's Government has decided that the Constitution of British Guiana must be suspended to prevent Communist subversion of the Government and a dangerous crisis both in public order and in economic affairs. . . . The faction in power have shown by their acts and their speeches that they are prepared to go to any lengths, including violence, to turn British Guiana into a Communist State. The Governor has therefore been given emergency powers

> and has removed the portfolios of the Party Ministers. Armed forces have landed to support the police and to prevent any public disorder which might be fomented by Communist supporters."

Then Sir Alfred Savage went on the air. He appealed to the police and volunteer forces "to carry out faithfully the tasks assigned to them". The British Navy and Army had come to back them up in protecting life and property and preserving public order. But, just to be on the safe side, Savage took away the guns of the local police !

My colleagues and I were relieved of our ministerial portfolios. The House of Assembly and the State Council were prorogued. The Governor was a virtual dictator. He was ruling with emergency powers.

All meetings were banned. Raids on the offices of the People's Progressive Party and the homes of Party leaders were immediately made. While I was still in my pyjamas, police raided my home, taking away papers, books and a recording machine—hoping, perhaps, to find secret directions from Malenkov ! But this was not all. Downstairs, the police were digging up the floor of my garage. When I asked why, the police drily smiled. They were looking for bombs !

Meanwhile, British soldiers—young lads—stood around my yard on guard. Looking at their faces, I found a queer expression ; a feeling of friendliness behind a tough exterior. It was as if they wanted to say : "This is none of our damned business. We were drafted against our will to do this dirty job." These boys had landed under the cover of darkness the day before, in battle formation, ready to kill and be killed. No doubt they were thoroughly indoctrinated on the subject of the "terrorists", "bandits" and "Communists". But meeting no resistance, they were overheard remarking later ; "Where's the war we came to fight ?"

Shots were fired, but not against these defenders of democracy. One was fired to break open the lock of our Party's office. And a salvo of guns—British guns—heralded the Governor's declaration of the suspension of the Constitution and the dismissal of Ministers.

Later in the same day I visited my office in the ministerial buildings. Police were everywhere. I must get the permission of the Governor before I could be admitted, I was told. When later I entered I found they had rifled my locked desk and taken many important papers.

From Wednesday onwards newsmen and cameramen appeared from all parts of the world. They hovered around my home, for, as one of them said, "the next move is yours". This was to them a strange crisis. No assemblies, no meetings, no marches, no shootings. A public meeting called by the Peace Committee for Wednesday was cancelled. No opportunity was to be given to the police to have a shooting spree.

The *Daily Herald* correspondent expressed the views of his colleagues when he wrote from Georgetown on October 9: "I flew into this crisis city of palms and wooden houses late last night. And this afternoon, 18 hours later, I am still looking for the crisis."

Little wonder that the correspondent could not find the crisis. For it was manufactured in Whitehall and Washington.

"Strange crisis this is," said the journalist to me. "In the midst of it a big international cricket match is going on!"

Even the slight heat generated during the week before had cooled off. On Thursday of the previous week the Speaker had refused to permit the suspension of standing rules and orders to allow the first reading of the Labour Relations Bill. Our members had walked out in protest. A mass meeting followed. I spoke to the Governor and later to the Speaker. The matter was settled—the Bill was taken on Monday of crisis week.

The crisis was greeted with mixed feelings. Among most of the Europeans, including the well-to-do Portuguese, there were expressions of jubilation. One sensed a difference here. But among the ordinary people there was first a feeling of bewilderment. The news had hit us as it had, no doubt, hit the world—like a bolt from the blue. But bewilderment soon changed into cold, resolute bitterness.

We issued a statement urging the people to remain "calm, quiet but firm".

The People's Progressive Party issued a circular headlined

"On Guard". The circular called for unswerving loyalty from our members. "Whatever happens in the next few days," it said, "let us remain firm and certain that if our leaders are arrested, new leaders will spring up. If our country is placed under martial law, let our people stay in their houses and go about their business in peace. Let us not be trapped in attempts to provoke us."

We called for a general strike. We called for non-violence, non-co-operation. Police seized leaflets and intimidated our printers. The Governor tried to counter our general strike call by declaring many occupations essential services. But the sugar workers came out on strike. Savings were being withdrawn from the postal savings banks. A boycott of British goods and stores owned by Booker's began. That the non-co-operation was being felt was proved by the Governor's frantic appeal for co-operation only a week after Black Friday.

The rape of democracy did not happen as quietly as our masters had hoped. In Britain, liberal opinion was roused and questioning. This was not like Malaya and Kenya. The Government had no opportunities for lurid, harrowing tales of looting, violence, terrorism and murder.

This was the uprooting by threat of bullets of a Government that had been democratically elected. Even though the bogey of Communism was raised, Labour opinion spoke in strong terms about "gunboat democracy" and said "the Government must prove its charges".

Mr. James Griffiths, former Colonial Minister, speaking at Portsmouth, called for specific evidence. He said: "It is for the Government to satisfy Parliament and the nation that this fear is well founded, not by vague and general allegations, but by evidence set out in specific terms."

The British Government announced that a White Paper on Guiana would be published and debated. It was in these circumstances that we decided to come to Britain. Mr. L. F. S. Burnham, the former Education Minister, and I were to put our case before the Government and the people.

There were rumours that we would not be allowed to leave British Guiana, but these the Government denied.

But while we were "free to leave", the gates were gradually closing. The Governments of Trinidad and Barbados told us we could not pass through their territories. The American vice-consul said he would give us neither visas nor transit permits for the U.S.A. The Dutch Government and the French Government would not permit us an overnight stay in Dutch Guiana or French Guiana—a necessary stage if we went by that route. The British and American air lines refused to carry us.

Finally we got out by chartering a plane—a large Dakota B.G.A. plane for just the two of us! This was expensive, but it was the only way, for voices in Britain were becoming insistent. We had been told the Universal Declaration of Human Rights, guaranteeing, among other things, freedom of movement, was applicable to everybody. But apparently it was only meant for the Chief Secretary and the favoured few. For no obstacle was placed in the way of the Chief Secretary. And Messrs. Fernandes, Carter, Luckhoo and Kendall, who supported the Government, went to England without trouble. But of course they were going to thank Her Majesty's Government and say what a wonderful thing had been done.

CHAPTER TWO

MAN-MADE DIFFICULTIES

"Guiana, whose rich feete are mines of golde,
Whose forehead knockes against the roofe of starres,
Stands on her tip-toes at faire England looking,
Kissing her hand, bowing her mightie breast,
And every signe of all submission making,
To be her sister and the daughter both,
Of our most sacred maide. . . ."

GEORGE CHAPMAN

"She is a region in Guiana, all gold and bounty."

WILLIAM SHAKESPEARE

British Guiana is the only British possession in the Continent of South America. It is sandwiched between Venezuela in the West, Brazil in the south-west and the south, Dutch Guiana in the east. Its coast line of about 270 miles borders the Atlantic Ocean.

There are a number of factors that explain the economic stagnation of this rich country, and I propose to outline some of them in this chapter.

From time to time, commissions, committees, experts and advisers have gone to British Guiana. Numerous reports have been written. But nearly always our imperialist sympathisers have been eager to point out that British Guiana is a "difficult" country with racial problems, drainage and irrigation problems, poor soil and so on. With all these difficulties we should, it seems, be thankful for the little progress that has been made. Imperialism has nothing to do with the problems, of course! And the sugar planters have really not arrested the growth of the country.

British Guiana is 83,000 square miles in area—nearly as large as Great Britain. About 86 per cent of this area is forest, 10 per cent savannah; the remainder, where nearly the whole population lives, forms the coastal belt, about 10 miles wide and mostly below sea level. Sea walls protect the capital, Georgetown, which is six feet below sea level.

Temperatures range from 75 to 90 degrees fahrenheit; Atlantic sea breezes and trade winds help to temper what would otherwise be a very humid equatorial climate. Rainfall is heavy.

The savannahs are generally 300 to 400 feet above sea level, but in the west, on the border with Brazil, the Pakarima Mountain is 9,000 feet, while in the south the Kanaku and Akarai are about 3,000 feet.

The hinterland is rich in resources. There are many varieties of timber; mineral resources include bauxite, gold, diamonds, tantalite, iron ore, manganese and valuable deposits of sands. Some geologists hold that British Guiana, being adjacent to oil-rich Venezuela and Trinidad, must have valuable deposits of oil.

To many, Guiana is "The Land of Glistening Waters". Four huge main rivers flow into the Atlantic. The Corentyne River forms the boundary with Dutch Guiana. The Berbice, Demerara and Essequibo rivers divide the country into, and give their names to, the three counties.

Georgetown stands at the mouth of the Demerara River, while the only other town, New Amsterdam, is on the mouth of the Berbice River. On the estuary of the Essequibo there are many huge islands, one being as large as the British Colony of Barbados. The rivers are navigable to ocean-going ships for 60 to 80 miles up stream.

Many races inhabit our country. British Guiana has been described as "The Land of Six Peoples". The British Guiana Constitution Commission, 1927, described the country as a "congeries of races from all parts of the world, with different instincts, different standards and different interests." The population is made up of Amerindians, Africans, East Indians, Portuguese, Chinese and Europeans.

In a population of 465,470 in December 1953, the distribution according to race groups was:

East Indians	215,260
Africans	165,090
Mixed or Coloured	51,200
Portuguese	8,340
European	4,050
Chinese	3,340
Amerindian	18,190

Before the arrival of foreigners, the Amerindians peopled this peaceful and beautiful country. English early adventurers of the 1530s and 1540s made numerous trading voyages to the Brazilian coast. But it was Sir Walter Raleigh, half a century later, who dreamed of "El Dorado" and planned the establishment of the English Empire in Guiana.

People were attracted by Raleigh's empire-building scheme. Successive groups of Englishmen attempted to settle along the Guiana coast, but the scheme ended for many of these people with the gallows. For James I was not prepared for trouble with Spain, and at that time Spain, dominant in South America, regarded Guiana as within her sphere.

In the wake of the British came Dutch and French adventurers. The Dutch succeeded in establishing themselves. They sailed up the rivers, set up trading posts and built protective forts. Kijk-over-al and Fort Zeelandia on the Essequibo still stand today as landmarks of their occupation.

At first, the emphasis was on trade with the Indian tribes. European trinkets and other trade goods were bartered for annato dye and cotton. But as the value of this trade declined, more and more emphasis was given to production of tobacco, and numerous small plantations began the production of tobacco, cotton, coffee, indigo, and, lastly, to a great extent, of sugar.

British planters came over from British Barbados and the nearby Caribbean Islands. They settled in Demerara, and by 1770 they were in the majority. British expeditionary forces set out from Barbados in 1796, captured it from the Dutch, to whom it was again ceded in 1802. But in 1803 it was retaken by the British and finally proclaimed a British possession in 1814.

Africans were brought back as slaves to work in the sugar plantations. They were transported not only to British Guiana, but also to other parts of the New World. Those were terrible days, and the slave trade a terrible business; it is conservatively estimated that nearly 10 million African slaves perished in the Middle Passage from West Africa to Guiana, the West Indies and the other thirteen British colonies in North America.

A British order-in-council of 1807 abolished the slave trade, but the traffic continued. Slavery was very profitable. Slaves were very cheap. I vividly recall a section of the Liverpool Exhibition which was set up as part of the Festival of Britain. It showed very clearly how the "triangular traffic" associated with slavery helped the development and growth of a prosperous Britain. A map showed a voyage of the slave ship *Ranger* from Liverpool to Anamoboe, West Africa, with a cargo of muskets, swords, gunpowder, pewter, cotton goods, trinkets and jewellery. From Anamoboe to Kingston, Jamaica, with slaves; from Kingston to Liverpool with coffee, cotton, coconuts, ginger, wine, rum and sugar. At every point in the triangle profit was made for the prosperity of Britain and particularly of its seaport towns, like Liverpool and Bristol.

The slaves protested against the inhuman treatment they received. Some ran away; others rebelled. The last rebellion was put down with great ferocity in 1812 when about 10,000 slaves rose in revolt. But despite the strong opposition of powerful vested interests—City elders, the Church (Bishop of Exeter) and admirals—the growing revolt of the slaves and the campaign carried on by the Abolition Society with the help of Buxton, Wilberforce and others, brought this traffic to an end.

The British Government soon abolished preference on sugar. At this point the planters faced a peculiar problem. They had to sell their sugar in the open market in competition with sugar produced by slave labour in Brazil and Cuba. Freed slaves were demanding 1s. a day. For the sugar industry to survive in its current form, for high profits to be maintained, cheap labour had to be found.

So the new system of indenture was started. Paper chains were substituted for iron chains; but they were just as binding. Indentured labour cost 1s. 2d. to 1s. 3d.—about the wage demanded by freed African slaves. Chinese were brought from China, and Portuguese from Madeira. These could not stand up to the rigours of plantation life. Later Indians came from India.

Sugar had become king, not only in Guiana but in the whole Caribbean . . . For 150 years of British rule we have had a typical colonial economy. The imperialists were never interested in developing a balanced economy. For most of the 150 years there has been a one-crop economy based on sugar. Despite the fact that we have a small population in a large country, where only 4 per cent of the land is cultivated, yet we have land hunger!

Many of our people continued to live on imported foods. We import flour, cheese, butter, powdered milk, meat, fish, peas, beans, jams, berries and so on. As this is a colonial country there is no manufacturing industry. There is only the extraction of our timber and our mineral resources—bauxite, gold, diamonds, tantalite . . . Urgent exploration is now in progress for manganese, iron ore, oil and radioactive thorium. Foreign capital, which is being encouraged by various concessions, is only interested in the exploitation and extraction of mineral resources.

We have no control of foreign trade. Consequently our trade is operated against our best interests. British Guiana is bound by a traditional policy of buying dear and selling cheap. The table below, taken from Dr. Benham's *National Income of British Guiana*, 1942, shows that while import prices increased from 1938 to 1943 by 136 per cent, export prices only increased by 32 per cent up to 1942, only to drop to 25 per cent in 1943.

	Import prices	Export prices
1938	100	100
1939	99.5	117
1940	130	119
1941	145	126
1942	194	132
1943	236	125

Taking 1938 as the base year, Dr. Neumark, the F.A.O. economist who toured the area in 1950 for the Caribbean Commission, estimated that the West Indies as a whole had to export 38 per cent and 36 per cent more sugar in 1947 to get the same quantities of flour and salted fish obtained in 1938.

Revaluation of our currency (the £ devaluation) made the situation even worse. Almost overnight our cost of living index jumped by about sixteen points.

We are not allowed to spend as many dollars as we earn. For instance, in 1951, \$31½ million of our exports went to the dollar areas, chiefly Canada. But we were allowed to import only $14½ million. Compare these figures with the export to Britain of $15 million and imports of $27 million.

There is a perpetual drain abroad by way of pensions, profits, interests and savings. Our two banks, the Royal Bank of Canada and Barclays Bank, and most of our insurance companies, are owned and operated by people abroad. Even our Post Office savings are placed in the hands of the Secretary of State for Colonies, for disposal at his discretion.

These, then, are some of the factors that govern our economy. They have nothing to do with "racial difficulties" or the country's geography. They are man-made; and they are made by alien control.

CHAPTER THREE

SUGAR-COATED GOVERNMENT

"When heavy droughts have come upon the land and the early and later rains have been withheld, and the crops have languished in the field, and the cane has refused to yield its abundant juice, they have cried out, 'the people are idle and they do not work'.

"When they turned the cattle of the estates into the Negroes' provision ground, tore the doors from the houses, applied the thumb-screw of rent to the last pinch, and drove the people to seek their own little freeholds, where, unmolested, they might cultivate and enjoy the fruits of the earth, the cry has still been, 'the people are idle, they will not work' . . . and they have forgotten that estates were never yet purchased as investment of capital, expected to yield a moderate but adequate interest, but on speculation in hope of yielding enormous return for an almost nominal outlay."

From the preface to the *Demerara Martyr,* the story of the REV. JOHN SMITH, written in 1848.

Sugar, we are told, is the sheet anchor of the economy of British Guiana. Destroy it and the Government will not be able to carry on and thousands of people will suffer. About one-third of the cultivated area of the country is devoted to this main crop. It constitutes more than 60 per cent of the colony's export trade. Herein lies at one and the same time the strength and power of the imperialists and the weakness of our economy.

Sugar has indeed played a major role in the agricultural economy of British Guiana, so much so that the history of British Guiana can truly be said to be the history of sugar. This history abounds with many instances of looting, bloodshed and murder. Dr. Eric Williams, a noted Caribbean historian, wrote in his *Capitalism and Slavery,* "Strange that an article like sugar, so sweet and necessary to human existence, should have occasioned so much crime and bloodshed". As late as 1948, five workers were killed and several others severely injured, at a plantation at Enmore.

Agricultural policy has always been determined not so much

"in conjunction with" sugar, but "after" sugar. Sugar has, indeed, been king. Sugar plantation owners are mostly absentee British business men. Three big sugar companies (English registered) operate in British Guiana—Booker Bros., McConnell and Co. Ltd.; Davson and Co. Ltd.; and the Demerara Co. Ltd.

Booker's is the largest of the three. It is the symbol of British imperialism in British Guiana. It is represented in all phases of economic life, so much so that British Guiana is sometimes colloquially referred to as "Booker's Guiana". This firm controls the greater part of the sugar estates, producing about 70 per cent of the whole output. It has twelve sugar plantations and eleven of the sixteen sugar factories.

Booker Bros. employs about 38,500 people; the firm has over fifty subsidiary companies in British Guiana and an interest in several other concerns. It has a dominant position in commerce, selling almost every conceivable product. Through Campbell, Booker, Carter it handles a large export and merchandising business. Booker's Stores has a huge general shop in Georgetown.

Unity Rum Merchants controls Booker's Rum Company and Albion Distilleries Ltd., both of which operate in British Guiana. There is also Booker's fleet of ships plying from Liverpool to Georgetown and between the West Indian Islands.

Not very long ago Booker's made tremendous profit by selling its extensive wood grant and saw mill interests to the Colonial Development Corporation. It has shares in the largest cattle company, the Rupununi Development Company, the chairman of which is a Booker director, Mr. E. G. Seaford. Sir F. J. Seaford, now a Booker's London director, was at one time a director of the Demerara Bauxite Company.

It is commonly said that Booker's owns everything except the funeral undertaking service. The people are exploited in every possible way; the only thing Booker's fails to do is to bury them.

The shareholders of Booker's include Atlas Assurance, Birmingham and District Investment Trust, Barclays Bank, London Life Assurance and so on.

Next to Booker's in importance in the sugar industry is the

Demerara Company, formed in 1891 by Sandbach Tinne and Co., the oldest family business in British Guiana. Its directors include Mr. I. R. Parker, great-great-grandson of one of the founders, and Mr. T. A. Taylor, of a Liverpool banking family. One of the company's largest shareholders is Lord Borwick of Hawkshead.

Davson and Co. Ltd. has three estates and one factory. The company is largely owned by the Davson family. Lieutenant-Colonel Harry M. Davson is the chairman, and among the shareholders are Lord Sinclair, Sir Geoffrey Davson and his father-in-law, Sir Rhys Williams, and the Dowager Lady Margot Davson.

These companies along with others in the British Caribbean are strongly buttressed by the powerful West Indian Committee in London. Their representatives have always been among the real rulers of our country.

I recall the appointment of Sir F. J. Seaford to the Legislative and Executive Councils after his defeat in the General Election of 1947. Mr. F. Morrish, of Sandbach Parker and Demerara Co. Ltd., replaced Sir F. J. Seaford when the latter left for the London office of Booker Bros. Mr. W. A. Macnie, managing director of the Sugar Producers' Association and one-time high Government official, subsequently replaced Mr. Morrish.

There are some members of the old Legislative Council (1947-53), nominated and elected, who have direct and indirect interests in the sugar industry. Mr. W. Raatgever and Mr. C. V. Wight, are shareholders of Schonard and Versailles Estates Ltd. C. V. Wight's father, Mr. P. C. Wight, is a director of Enmore Estates Ltd. Nominated member G. H. Smellie is a shareholder of Enmore Estates Ltd., and a former director of Davson and Co. Ltd. Another nominated member, Cyril Farnum, is secretary of Humphrey and Co. Ltd.

In the new Council nominated by the Government after we were removed from office, W. Raatgever, G. H. Smellie, Cyril Farnum and W. A. Macnie have all found places—but not because they were elected.

Apart from indirect representation in the Legislative Council, the sugar interests have their representatives in important positions on various statutory boards and committees—Drainage Board, Central Board of Health, Transport and Harbours, Local Government Board, and so on.

This political power permits the sugar planters to determine major questions of policy involving their own interests. Once the policy is decided it is inevitably put into effect. The dividing line between policy making and administration is obscure. The fact is that Governorships and high administrative positions in the Colonial Empire are merely big jobs for the British civil servants. Those who do not toe the line simply do not get the big jobs. In British Guiana the civil servants have sense enough to know that if they are to get promotion they cannot "buck" against King Sugar. Actually, many ex-civil servants hold prominent positions directly and indirectly associated with sugar.

The labour problem and how the sugar estate owners attempt to solve it is a most instructive theme. About the oldest headache of the sugar planters has been the problem of securing and maintaining an adequate and surplus labour force providing them with cheap manpower.

At first, African slavery provided the answer. After the abolition of slavery the sugar planters turned to indentured immigrants (five-year contract slaves) from Madeira, China and India. But unfortunately for the sugar planters, the indenture system ceased in 1917. Later attempts at settling Assyrians and displaced Jews failed. Other means, therefore, had to be found, particularly after 1917, not only to maintain the necessary and surplus labour force, but also to compensate for the drift from the plantations.

These measures have taken different forms—lack of agricultural diversification, prevention of the use of land, deliberately inadequate drainage and irrigation on land outside the areas of the sugar estates, price-fixing of wages and farmers' produce. One measure—control of malaria—has even taken on a humanitarian garb.

Malaria, coupled with malnutrition, was largely responsible for the reduction of the population. The 1949 Annual Report of British Guiana said :

> "Between 1838, when slavery was abolished, and 1917, when the last batch of immigrants arrived, British Guiana had obtained more than 430,000 colonists from India, Africa, Madeira, China and other places. Even making allowances for immigrants returning to their native lands, it might be assumed that they would have maintained their numbers. Yet the population of 309,000 in 1911 had become 307,000 in 1921."

If the sugar workers were to remain alive—dead men produce no profits—some means had to be found to wipe out malaria. Dr. Giglioli, medical adviser to the Sugar Producers' Association, showed in the 1946 Annual Report for British Guiana how the use of D.D.T. had brought the infantile mortality rate down in a most dramatic way and how the birth rate had risen. At the same time malaria among school children dropped from 60 per cent between 1938 and 1945 to 18 per cent in 1946.

British Guiana has a population density of about five persons for each square mile, compared with 1,246 in Barbados and 613 in Grenada. Yet the farmers are land hungry.

The last census disclosed that the average farmer had 3¾ acres of land—and this badly drained and irrigated. But 15-20 acres of well drained and well irrigated land is, according to experts, necessary to provide a decent livelihood. The fact that land has not been available accounts for our various food shortages. Local cooking oil and fats have been scarce for a good many years, with the exception of the period immediately after the 1950 floods. The shortage became so acute in 1948-49 that about $70,000 of precious Canadian hard currency had to be spent for the import of Canadian soya bean oil. In 1952 large quantities of oil had to be imported from Holland and Trinidad. If land had been readily available to the farmers during past years, thousands of them could easily have cultivated at least three to five acres each in coconuts. Coconut shortage means not only curtailment of oil, but also of copra meal production. Shortage of oil and copra meal in turn affects the soap, pig and dairy industries.

On the Essequibo coast, sometimes referred to as the "blighted" coast, most of the farmers have only a few acres of land. And this is mostly sown in rice. Since rice is a seasonal crop it means that the greater part of the population is not fully occupied for most of the year. This is the main reason for the depressed state of affairs on the Essequibo coast, and not, as is sometimes said, the breaking down of the Essequibo sugar estates. It is sugar which is really responsible not only for the blighted conditions of the Essequibo but other parts of the country as well. So far as the sugar planters are concerned there must be no prosperity outside the sugar estates, lest their labour force be attracted away.

Large tracts of land are kept idle or are not properly utilised. The sugar planters control directly about 170,000 acres, and tax figures for 1950 showed that more than 50 per cent of the total land holdings were uncultivated. This land idleness can be maintained because the rent charged by the Government averages only five cents an acre for nearly 90,000 acres of land. In 1951 I introduced in the Legislative Council a motion which sought to withdraw the leases or to tax uncultivated land held by the sugar planters. This was defeated.

Why control land in such large holdings and not beneficially cultivate them? The answer is to be found in a deliberate restrictive policy to maintain a large surplus labour force round the sugar estates. The plots of one acre and half an acre given to the workers for farming are just enough to keep them from becoming too disgruntled with their insecurity and low wages and to keep them from migrating during the periods of seasonal unemployment. Too much land must not be given, apparently, lest the workers become economically self-sufficient and independent.

To force the sugar workers to abandon their more profitable rice and provision farming and to provide the sugar estates with more days of work a week, the sugar planters resorted to the confiscation of land. Between 1943 and 1947 approximately 2,000 acres of rice land and 1,000 acres of provision land were taken away from the resident workers.

In 1944 the King Report *On Certain Questions in Connection with Piece Work on Sugar Estates* said: ". . . the reason why available work is not fully taken up is because resident workers find it more profitable to work on their own rice fields and farms and some non-residents have left working on the fields on the estates for more profitable occupations."

In 1948, the Report of the Labour Department disclosed that the average number of days worked was higher on the East Bank, Demerara, than in other parts of the country. "This," it added, "may be due to the greater dependence on earnings on the East Bank, owing to the absence of rice and farmlands in this area".

Closely associated with land control and land hunger is the major problem of drainage and irrigation.

According to the Royal Commission's report of 1945, ". . . practically all well drained land is in sugar . . . . The areas devoted to rice and pasture are badly drained and abound in large swampy areas where almost amphibious cattle, sheep and pigs eke out an unusual existence".

The sugar planters have always controlled drainage and irrigation policy. Sir F. J. Seaford was for many years chairman of the Drainage Board. He was succeeded by Mr. F. Morrish of the Demerara Co. Ltd., who on his retirement was replaced by Mr. W. Macnie, managing director of the Sugar Producers' Association.

It is true the Government engaged Mr. F. Hutchinson to advise on drainage and irrigation, and that thousands of dollars have been voted for preliminary surveys. But it is equally true that the planters vigorously opposed Mr. Hutchinson's comprehensive drainage and irrigation schemes.

Mr. Hutchinson and the sugar planters did not look on drainage and irrigation from the same point of view. Mr. Hutchinson, realising that the industrialisation of British Guiana is something far in the future, believed that only thousands of additional acres of well drained, properly irrigated land could raise the standard of living and solve the growing unemployment problem.

Farmers are every year being urged to increase their productivity. In 1951 the Financial Secretary pointed to the Fletcher Committee's report which showed that of a rise of 14 points in the cost-of-living index between 1949 and October 1950 only

4.1 points were due to the rise in the cost of foreign products. What he did not say was that the floods of early 1950 were mainly responsible.

In the struggle between Mr. Hutchinson and the sugar planters the administration sided with sugar. Frustrated, Mr. Hutchinson left the colony. He had planned colony-wide water control schemes, estimating that on the present rate of population increase all arable and cultivable lands would be taken up in seventeen years if 25 acres were given to each family. Therefore he wanted all the schemes to be taken up immediately.

The sugar planters have opposed Mr. Hutchinson's schemes for two reasons. First, because they will make too much drained and irrigated land available too quickly. Second, because they will cost the sugar kings more money.

The sugar planters are, of course, interested in the marketing and price-fixing of farmers' produce and also wage-fixing in industrial and commercial undertakings. The reason is obvious. For when a worker leaves a sugar estate he must seek other employment or become a peasant farmer ; if neither is attractive he must remain where he is, so wages and the price of farm produce must be kept low.

It is in this light that opposition to legislation enforcing a minimum wage must be regarded. When in 1950 I introduced a minimum wage motion in the Legislative Council, I was supported by only four members.

What of price control? Consider the Rice Marketing Board, where real power is in the hands of Government nominees. This body is composed of eight Government nominees and eight rice producers, the present chairman being a Government nominee.

The Rice Marketing Board was ostensibly created to eliminate the middle-men, the merchants who were exploiting the rice growers. But the real reason was to prevent the rise in the prices of export rice to $20 and $25 a bag, reached during the First World War, and the consequent drift from sugar to rice production.

The price of our rice has for a long time been about half the world price. For instance :

	dollars		
	1946	1947	1948
U.S.A.	215.54	247.77	364.66
Brazil	179.00	200.17	234.70
British Guiana	105.52	115.61	115.96

It is conservatively estimated that the rice farmers have lost $10 million to $15 million since the Board came into existence.

This, no doubt, is why in 1950 exemption from price control by the Rice Marketing Board was granted to a company to be formed jointly by the British Government's Colonial Development Corporation and the British Guiana Government. For the Colonial Development Corporation could not see itself competing successfully for labour against the sugar planters if it had to sell its rice through a Board in which sugar held a strong position. It wanted to produce and sell rice with a free hand.

This aroused tremendous opposition from the rice peasants and the progressive politicians. Obviously there should not be two different laws for different sets of interests. The Rice Marketing Board should be abolished or reformed to protect the interests of all. In mid-1951 the Legislative Council nevertheless rejected a motion to abolish the Rice Marketing Board and replace it by a similar single selling body, democratically and co-operatively controlled by the rice peasants.

Later the Colonial Development Corporation decided there was not much to be gained by entering the rice industry. Instead it took the safer course of lending the Rice Development Company $5 million at ¾ per cent higher interest than the rate at which it borrows from the British Treasury.

The sugar planters also sit in the Government Marketing Committee which fixes the minimum guaranteed prices for farm produce. The prices are generally fixed at a low level, with the result that farmers find it difficult to make a living. Government officials argue that in times of glut the Government Produce Depot loses a great deal of money and that if prices were higher the losses would be greater.

In case non-availability of land with consequent high rentals, poor drainage and irrigation, low farm produce prices and poor wages are not sufficient to make the sugar worker remain in and around the sugar estates, a new method has been devised.

Nuclear housing schemes are the new method. The sugar planters calculate that there are 5,262 families of essential workers and 6,555 families of non-essential part-time and occasional workers. They have said they are prepared to house the essential workers. For the non-essential workers 9,334 house lots have been prepared on the front lands. In some cases loans were generously provided by the estates. Now the Government-appointed Sugar Industry Welfare Fund Committee is making loans available from the Sugar Industry Fund.

The effect is to tie workers, even though non-essential, round the estates, and at the same time to take the opportunity of entering directly into the field of profitable landlordism.

The leases to be signed by the workers contain restrictions preventing the planting of fruit and rearing of animals, ostensibly on grounds of health, but in fact limiting the economic self-sufficiency of the tenants. An annual rent of $2.88 is charged. This is a very profitable affair. The rent for 1,228 acres on which it is proposed to lay out 9,334 houses totals $28,293 a year. Compare this with the 5 cents an acre paid to the Government by the sugar companies for leased lands.

The sugar planters are making huge profits. They forever tell us that sugar does not pay, but their balance sheets prove the opposite. Between 1948 and 1950 Booker's net profits after tax rose from £207,455 to £385,453. In 1951 the combined net profit was £660,677. With amounts deducted for tax, minority interests and reserves the total in 1951 was £2,237,904. And this figure is arrived at after deducting the high salaries paid to directors and high officials.

We of the People's Progressive Party have been accused of wanting to destroy the sugar industry. This has never been and never will be the policy of the P.P.P. But we are thoroughly opposed to the present system and the present organisation of the industry, by which the workers are sweated and millions of dollars produced by them go into the pockets of sugar kings in England.

The wealth produced in the industry must be better distributed so that the workers get decent living standards. Proper planning to take care of the seasonal unemployed, tied and surplus sugar workers, must be an immediate and urgent objective, both in the interests of the workers and of British Guiana.

This reorganisation can take two forms : complete nationalisation or reforms. Nationalisation of the sugar industry, and indeed of all major industries, is our ultimate objective. In the interim, while British Guiana is still tied to British imperialism, with limited constitutional powers, certain reforms should be undertaken to break the back of imperialism.

Professor Arthur Lewis in his paper *Issues in Land Settlement* wrote of the sugar industry :

> "New forms of reorganisation must be tried and must be tried urgently. In Puerto Rico the Government has shown itself alive to the fact, and is greatly to be praised for taking the initiative in experimenting with the Proportional Profit Farm.
>
> "In the British territories, on the other hand, Governments are content to meet a succession of disturbances with a succession of commissions of enquiry. This is not good enough. . . . New forms must be created which will take the West Indian sugar industry 'out of politics' in the sense of earning general acceptance, or the West Indian community will sooner or later simply tear itself to pieces and destroy the sugar industry in the process."

In Puerto Rico no estate is permitted to hold more than 500 acres. The excess lands were bought by the Government and distributed. Individual families got up to 25 acres. Proportional profit farms (workers getting wages and sharing profits) and co-operatives were also set up.

In another paragraph of the same report Professor Lewis, referring to the system of farming in Fiji, says:

> "Some people believe that this is the system that will eventually supply the West Indies with a solution to the problems of the sugar industry. A large-scale agency will plough the land, control irrigation, supply seedlings and fertilisers, organise harvesting and operate factories, while peasants will plant and cultivate the crop on their own account, subject to charges for services performed. The

peasants will have a representative council, but this will not take over the functions of the agency. In Fiji and in the Sudan the agency has been a private company, but it might equally well be a public corporation, as it is now to be in the Sudan."

Even under the Fiji system the workers would be much better off in British Guiana than they are now. When the Venn Commission visited British Guiana I submitted a memorandum showing the profits earned by the sugar producers. I calculated the average cost of growing one acre of sugar cane. I found from figures supplied to me by workers, drivers and book-keepers, that the average price paid to the labourers for planting, reaping and transporting one acre of cane was $86.89 in 1948. For manure, mules, oxen, punts, etc., the average cost an acre was $33.24. Taking the price paid in 1948 to cane farmers for canes supplied to the estates, the average yield an acre was $243.33. On this basis the rate of exploitation was about 142 per cent. In other words, in a 10-hour day the workers were paid for only about four hours and they gave about six hours of free labour to the sugar planters.

Sugardom is not only exploiting the sugar industry; it is ruining the whole colony. The time has come when the sugar-coated Government should be replaced by a People's Government.

CHAPTER FOUR

BELOW HUMAN DECENCY

"I do not believe that anybody who has not seen it with his own eyes, can begin to imagine the poverty in which so many of our fellow citizens of the Commonwealth are condemned to live."

JAMES GRIFFITHS, former Colonial Secretary, in October 1951.

"The fundamental problem of the colonial people is their intense poverty, from which stem all the ills of colonial society. It is the problem of perpetual hunger, of death from preventable diseases, and starvation; of illiteracy fostered by the ruling powers to assure a constant supply of cheap and docile labour for land, mine and plantation owners."

KUMAR GHOSHAL, *People in the Colonies*

British Guiana is sometimes referred to as the Magnificent Province. For a few, imperialist rule has indeed made it a magnificent province with a pleasant and abundant life. But for the masses of workers and farmers it has been a life of destitution, misery and want. There is evidence of this everywhere.

A few years ago Professor MacMillan, in his book, *Warning from the West Indies,* wrote: "Any social and economic study of the West Indies is . . . necessarily a study of poverty." In *Democracy and Empire in the Caribbean,* Paul Blanchard, a former U.S. State Department official, said:

> "The labouring population of almost the whole area lives at a level below human decency. The outward signs of Caribbean poverty . . . ragged clothing, bare feet, children with bloated bellies, shacks made of flattened cans, and lines of unemployed workers waiting at closed gates."

The situation has not changed much since these words were written. Any change, however, has been for the worse. The Indian Commissioner to the West Indies, S. M. Sahay, who in early 1951 visited British Guiana, Trinidad and Jamaica, the then largest developed territories, came to the same conclusion. He said the thing most common to the three territories was poverty.

Miss Elsa Hagland, Home Economist of the Food and Agricultural Organisation of the United Nations, told our legislators in December 1952 that she had rarely seen such "terrific signs of malnutrition", and she was "shocked to her bones". And all this chiefly in the Corentyne, which is supposed to be the most healthy and prosperous part of British Guiana.

Here is an extract from the evidence of a sugar worker before the Venn Commission of Inquiry into the Sugar Industry of British Guiana:

> "*Chairman*: What do you want to tell us?
>
> "*Indian Witness*: We have to walk about five or six miles every day to get to work on the back-dam. We leave home at six o'clock to start work seven or eight o'clock and work until five or six o'clock.
>
> "*Chairman*: Do you work all the year round at that distance from your home, or only now and then?
>
> "*Witness*: I walk that distance most of the time.
>
> "*Chairman*: Is that your main complaint?
>
> "*Witness*: No, I have no rice-field, no cow and no money. I live on the estate in a range and do estate work. Since I came to the Colony I have been doing that work.
>
> "*Chairman*: How much did you earn last week?
>
> "*Witness*: I earn from 5 dollars to 10 dollars a week, but as I am now an old man I cannot earn more than 5 dollars to 7 dollars a week, which is insufficient. The week I buy clothes, I cannot buy rations."

In 1942 a cost of living survey was carried out by a Government-appointed committee in Albouystown, a working class area in Georgetown. It showed that the average working class family of 4.6 persons earned a total income of $7.41 but spent $8.23 a week.

The weekly income did not consist wholly of wages, but was also made up of such things as loans, pensions, poor relief, rent and so on, nearly 20 per cent of the total of $7.41. Under the capitalist-imperialist régime, therefore, even with charities and doles, the working people cannot balance their low-standard budgets. The explanation of the fact that expenditure exceeded income is that people owed rent to landlords and money to shopkeepers from whom they were buying on credit. They were living through one week on the anticipated earnings of the next.

The expenditure of $8.07 (a dollar is worth 4s. 2d.) a week was made as follows:

Food	$4.58
Clothing	$1.07
Rent	$1.07
Fuel and light	47 cents
Other items	$1.04

How well did people eat? Dr. Francis, then Government Medical Officer, tells us:

> "The food available represented 2,134.4 calories daily per man value. The technical Commission on Nutrition of the League of Nations has placed the calory requirements per man value to be 2,400 calories of food actually assimilated for an individual not engaged in actual work. Moreover, the diet is not well balanced, as carbohydrates bulk very largely, while the percentage of protein and fat are low. Sufficient of the protein is not derived from animal origin."

How about the children? The Government's Ten-year Planning Report (1948) is revealing. Appended to the Report is a memorandum from the semi-official Nutrition Committee which says:

> "As a result of sampling surveys in widely scattered areas, we can affirm that at least 25 per cent of schoolchildren are necessitous."

This early nutritional deficiency in childhood leads later to disease, high mortality and low expectancy of life. Infant and maternal mortality rates are high. Here is a comparison: the infantile mortality rate per 1,000 is 32 in the United Kingdom, 31 in the U.S.—and as high as 86 in British Guiana.

Tuberculosis increased from 215 cases in 1947 to 532 in 1949;

hospital waiting lists for the Best Hospital jumped from 329 at the end of 1949 to 548 at the end of 1951.

Then there is the housing disgrace. The Cost of Living Survey found that the average number of persons per room was 2.6, but in some instances as many as twelve people lived in a single tenement room.

The housing conditions get worse. In Georgetown, which houses about one-fifth of British Guiana's population, slum conditions are widespread. Many houses have fallen down. I remember one that tilted for some time and finally toppled over one evening. People had continued to live there because they had no other shelter. When the house fell fifty people were inside.

About 18 per cent of the population live on the sugar plantations, mostly in dilapidated, barrack-type "ranges" built during the days of slavery. Here is a description from the Venn Commission's report:

> "In quite a number the corrugated iron roofs were leaking and the fabric of the buildings was in a general state of decay. In numerous instances temporary sheets of awnings have been fixed over the beds to keep off the rain. They had mud floors and, consequently, with the rain dripping from the roofs, these were made slippery and dangerous; in many cases we found bags laid over the floor to prevent slipping. They are built without any plan on low-lying, uneven ground. There are few, if any, proper footpaths, and in rainy weather communication is difficult.
>
> "The common latrines, often built over drainage trenches, are frequently in a bad state of repair, with little privacy."

Imagine the state of sanitation, and the conditions of the sugar estate workers during the heavy rainfall and flood periods which are frequent. The whole housing area becomes covered with polluted water from the overflowing latrine trenches. This water remains on the land for days and sometimes weeks, during which time boats and canoes have to be used.

In contrast, the quarters of the manager and the officers are usually dry. During the 1950 floods I went to the manager at Lusignan to request that the workers' housing area be properly empoldered and a pump used to get rid of the polluted water. His first reply was to ask me whether I knew I was trespassing —and this in my own constituency. The pump was never provided.

Four houses built in the compound of the Agriculture Department for senior Government officials are estimated to have cost more than $96,000.

In British Guiana we need not only a decent standard of living, better housing and fair distribution of land: we need also a thorough overhaul of the education system.

Primary education is free, but the schools are almost all under-staffed, under-equipped and over-crowded. The Ten-Year Planning Report of 1948 admitted that there were then about 13,000 children between six and fourteen years of age who did not attend school.

The 1951-52 report on Primary Education Policy said it was not uncommon to find 800 children admitted to a school designed for 400. The report added:

> "Classes of 60 rapidly swell in number to 80 and 90; and classes over 90 are not uncommon. Under these impossible conditions education tends to become a mere mockery..."

The Venn Commission said: "The story of too many children for the physical capacity of the school, and of too many pupils in a class was the same wherever we went."

The effects of the poor educational facilities are shown in the widespread illiteracy which reaches 49.55 per cent among the Amerindians and 44.02 per cent among the East Indians, who constitute nearly 42 per cent of the population. But in spite of this the Government in 1951 appointed the Nicole Committee to investigate how to provide educational facilities within the limits of the present financial education vote which shows a tendency to rise. Or in other words, how to cut down the present inadequate standards.

The working class cannot afford secondary education, which has to be paid for—books, fees and so on. In the words of the Director of Education, "no grammar school education is or can be provided for 99 per cent of elementary school children".

The Cost of Living Survey, 1942, showed that the average

family spent about 14 cents (9d.) a week on medical attention and medicines. But the consultation fee charged by a doctor varied from $2 (8s. 4d.) to $5 (£1 0s. 10d.). This meant that the majority of working people had to resort to the medical services provided at the public hospitals which were, and still are, under-staffed and under-equipped. Treatment and care is in direct proportion to the ability to pay. Workers generally enter not as paying patients, but as "paupers" and "poverty" cases. The latter pay a small fee and enjoy the dubious benefit of wearing their own and not Government-provided pyjamas.

At times, patients have to sleep on the floor for want of beds at the Georgetown Public Hospital. On these occasions the patients with beds usually surrender their mattresses to the patients on the floor. The patients with beds then sleep on a blanket over the springs. During the cold, rainy weather I found that some patients did not have adequate blankets.

* * *

The analysis in this chapter is based mainly on the report of the Cost of Living Survey, 1942. But the cost of living has been rising steadily since 1938. In 1942, according to the Survey, the cost of living was about 60 per cent more than in 1938, but:

> "There is no doubt that the standards of living have undergone considerable deterioration since the outbreak of the war . . . and that the percentage increase in the cost of living would have been greater had the statistics been based on the cost of maintaining the 1938 standards of living."

According to the Colonial Office Report of 1951, the latest year for which figures are available, prices then stood at 261 per cent of the 1938 level.

From time to time since 1942, increases in wages have been made to Government employees, but, as usual, not until real wages had dropped to such a level that pressure from working people could no longer be resisted. Whenever wages caught up with the cost of living, they were always so fixed as merely to maintain the miserable standards prevailing in 1938 and 1942.

Though the cost of living is almost as high as in Britain, these were the wages in private industry, where wages are lower than in Government employ:

	Resident	*Non-Resident*
	£ s. d.	£ s. d.
Sugar industry:		
Field workers: male	1 17 6	2 0 6
„ „ female	16 7½	18 5½
	Unskilled	*Skilled*
Factory workers: male	2 0 1	2 19 0
„ „ female	19 3	
Bauxite industry:	2 16 0	3 16 0
Garment industry:		
Georgetown	2 7 6	3 3 9
Other areas	2 0 0	2 14 9
Port labour:	2 10 0	3 18 0
Rice labour:		
Men	- - -	2 7 3
Women	1 3 1	
Government Service:		
Male, Georgetown	2 8 6	
„ rural areas	2 0 9	
Female, Georgetown	1 15 9	
„ rural areas	1 10 6	

There is no comprehensive social insurance scheme providing for sickness, unemployment and retirement benefits. The miserable sum of $1.50 a month (6s. 3d.) is given as poor relief to the indigent and unemployed.

Old age pensioners must reach the age of 65 and pass a means test before they can qualify for an allowance of $5,00 (20s. 10d.) and $3.50 (14s. 7d.) a month for town and country respectively. If the pensioner's monthly income exceeds $3.50 a month the allowance is not granted.

A motion seeking to abolish the means test and to reduce the qualifying age for a pension to 55 was defeated by the Legislative Council. An amendment seeking to reduce the age limit to 60, although accepted by the Legislative Council, has not yet been put into force by the Government. The means test is now being revised upwards to $10 a month.

Meanwhile, unemployment and crime is on the increase. Many who cannot find work are resorting to stealing. Expenditure on police and prisons is mounting. An expenditure of half a million dollars in 1940 for the police has jumped to about $1,800,000 in 1953.

CHAPTER FIVE

HOW WE CAME TO OFFICE

"All over the world the ordinary people are challenging the entrenched positions of the privileged, and are organising and fighting to win rights that have so long been withheld from them."

PAUL ROBESON

"We have made the fire but have stopped the chimney."

CHARLES BULLER

In the face of perpetual misery and degradation, of terror and bloodshed, there developed among the working people a growing trade union and political consciousness.

Their experience of sugar rule impelled them to struggle and organise. They had known not the sweetness of sugar, only the bitterness.

It was in British Guiana, in 1922, that there was organised the first trade union in any colonial country of the British Empire—the British Guiana Labour Union. Then in the middle of the world economic depression of 1931, came the British Guiana Workers' League. By 1939 there were ten trade union organisations. The sugar workers were organised in the British Guiana Workers' League and the Man-Power Citizens' Association. The British Guiana Labour Union had a large following, particularly among the dock workers. In 1941 the British Guiana Trades Union Council was formed, affiliating the various trade unions.

The employers at first refused to recognise the Man-Power Citizens' Association, but the growing militancy of the workers forced them to concede. Their policy then was to divide the workers into racial and industrial compartments. The Workers' League was recognised for factory workers, who were predominantly African; the Man-Power Citizens' Association was recognised for the field workers, who were predominantly Indian.

This weakness in the trade union movement became noticeable towards the end of the war. The Trades Union Council, however, attempted by a process of amalgamation and demarcation to prevent disunity.

In 1948 was formed the Guiana Industrial Workers' Union which soon gathered a very strong following among the sugar workers—but the planters refused to negotiate with this union. Strikes in the sugar industry became frequent.

The workers had always lacked political support. Effective political power was in the hands of the sugar planters and other interests. Throughout the whole of the nineteenth century and the early part of this century there was a virtual planters' oligarchy. The franchise was severely limited. In 1910 only 11,000 of a population of over 300,000 had the right to vote. This right was enjoyed mostly by the pure whites and the mixed coloured. Indians and Africans were denied any part in the political life of the country.

But out of the plantations and the fields came a growing number, particularly of Africans, who acquired education and joined the middle class. These provided clerical personnel in Government and commercial services; they also went into the independent professions, particularly law and medicine. It was from this middle class group that insistent demands were made for constitutional reforms.

In 1928 a reform of the Constitution took place. A Legislative Council was set up; it was composed of twenty-nine members—ten who were officials, nineteen non-official. Of the non-official members fourteen were elected and five were chosen by the Governor. So the elected members were in a minority. The franchise was severely restricted, hedged in with income and property qualifications. The majority of Indian and Negro workers were excluded from the right to vote.

But the composition of the Executive Council, which was the policy-making body, was significant. This consisted of the Governor as chairman, six officials and six non-officials who were appointed by the Governor—not elected—from the Legislative Council. Two of the non-officials selected by the Governor were elected members of the Legislative Council.

This Constitution clearly placed all effective power in the hands of the Governor and his officials.

The then Liberal Party, dominated by the middle class leaders, agitated for further constitutional advances. The economic depression of the 1930s and the mass discontent in the Caribbean brought to the area a Royal Commission which recommended, among other things, constitutional reforms.

In 1943 a new Constitution was granted. I deliberately use the word "granted". For the constitutions are not instruments of our own creation. They are given and taken by Orders-in-Council signed by the reigning monarch in Britain.

The Legislative Council was to have fourteen elected members, seven nominated and three officials. But elections under this Constitution were postponed until November 1947. The war was given as an excuse. The real fear was that despite the severely restricted franchise, the general agitation throughout the country would have thrown up new elected members.

The old elected members were allowed to continue. The militancy of the workers, however, forced the Governor to nominate to the Legislative Council Ayube Edun, president of the Man-Power Citizens' Association, and H. N. Critchlow, general secretary of the British Guiana Labour Union.

Many factors contributed to the general political awakening of this period. Students and ex-servicemen were returning home. Many of the students had been to the United States and worked their way through colleges and universities; the ex-servicemen had been recruited from the working class and the unemployed. These were imbued with the spirit of the Atlantic Charter, with the struggle for freedom and independence which had assumed a world-wide character.

Towards the end of 1943, I returned with my wife to British Guiana. She had been active in progressive student life at Detroit and Wayne universities. My seven years in the United States were for me a political awakening. Two years at Howard University in Washington D.C. brought me into touch with the American colour bar. I became interested in the Indian struggle for independence. Pandit Jawaharlal Nehru's autobiography *Towards Freedom* was a political inspiration. While studying dentistry at North Western University Dental School in Chicago, I found the time to read economics, sociology, philosophy and political science at evening classes and summer school.

Like others, we joined in the struggle, at first contributing articles and writing letters to the press on significant political events. In 1945 I became treasurer of the Man-Power Citizens' Association. In 1946 five of us, including H. J. M. Hubbard, then secretary of the British Guiana T.U.C., organised the Political Affairs Committee. We issued a free monthly monographed bulletin called *P.A.C.*, which soon became a bugbear of the planters. Insistent appeals were made in the Legislative Council, and once in the House of Commons, for the banning of *P.A.C.*

A year later the Women's Political and Economic Organisation was formed under the leadership of Winifred Gaskin and Janet Jagan. Among other activities, it particularly agitated for the unrestricted right of women to vote. Until the 1953 elections, many women—housewives who had no income and owned no property, and domestic workers who earned less than $10 a month—did not have the vote.

In 1947, general elections were fought for the first time under the 1943 Constitution. There was no real political party. The Liberal Party of the 1920s, dominated by the middle class and professional people, had died. A Labour Party was got together for electioneering purposes, but it dissolved soon after the elections.

Opposed to our growing working class movement were two racialist organisations. The reactionary East Indians worked through the East Indian Association and the Africans through the League of Coloured Peoples—appealing to the racialist sentiment of the two major race groups.

The British had played well the familiar imperialist game of divide and rule. They learnt from the experiences of the Dutch. In the early days of slavery and slave revolts it was the Amerindians who were used as policemen and who used to hunt down runaway slaves. The Waddington Constitution report underlined this. It pointed out that the "Indians, as a sort of militia or police, became a necessary part of the machinery of government", and a famous Dutch Governor was able, "by working in close co-operation with the Indian tribes, especially the warlike Caribs, to strengthen the security of the colony against Spanish encroachment and slave rebellion".

After the abolition of slavery, East Indians were brought to work the plantations. They were paid one-third to one-half the wages demanded by Africans.

So there started an early hostility between the two races. Many of the freed African slaves migrated to the neighbouring plantation areas and set up villages. The more prosperous of them entered the professions; others became civil servants; the less fortunate drifted into the police and other Government undertakings. The Government services became a near-monopoly of Africans, except, of course, for the principal administrative posts which were reserved for Europeans.

In the new situation under the British, therefore, it was the Africans who became the "necessary part of the general machinery of government". Whenever sugar workers were shot in the sugar plantations, whether at Enmore, Ruimveldt, or Leonora, it was inevitably African policemen shooting Indian workers.

The appeal of the racialist politicians was simple enough.

The Indian politicians told Indian workers that only they could get the workers the Government jobs which were now being denied to them in favour of the Africans. But first, said the politicians, they must be elected to the Legislative Council. They agitated for universal adult suffrage. For in addition to the income and property qualifications, there was a literacy test for the franchise which debarred many Indians from voting, since about 40 per cent of the Indian population were illiterate.

In this sense the Indian politicians were progressive. But their progressiveness was limited, since many of them, like their African middle class counterparts, were not prepared to abolish the property ($500) or income ($100 a month) qualifications for eligibility to contest a seat at the elections.

African leadership, on the other hand, wanted to maintain its strategic posts in the machinery of government. The weapon of these leaders was fear. They told the African electors that the Indians had not only become big landlords and business men but were also filling the professions, and if the Africans did not support each other as a race they would soon lose the only thing they had left—their jobs. They were opposed to universal adult suffrage without a literacy test—Africans are almost 100 per cent literate.

As a result of all this, the cause of the working class was not pursued militantly. There was need for unity and proper direction.

As a member of the Legislative Council, I saw soon after the elections in 1947 the necessity for bringing together all the progressive elements into one party which would not pursue a racial line but would fight on class lines, advancing a programme on behalf of all working people against the planters and vested interests. From the Political Affairs Committee formed by us in 1946 to demand constitutional and other reforms, the People's Progressive Party was born in January 1950. This party succeeded in uniting all the racial groups, and it launched a vigorous campaign.

In 1950 the Labour Government sent out the Waddington Commission to take evidence and recommend changes in the Constitution—the growing demands of the Guianese people could no longer be ignored. The chairman was Sir John Waddington, former Acting Governor of British Guiana. Professor V. Harlow and Dr. Rita Hinden were the two other members of the Commission.

The Waddington Commission recommended that the limited franchise based on a literacy, property and income test be swept away ; and that full adult suffrage and a two-chamber legislative system be introduced. Provision was made for a lower house, the House of Assembly, and an upper house, the State Council.

The House of Assembly was to have 24 elected members, together with three ex-officio members. The State Council had nine members—six nominated by the Governor directly and three others appointed by him on the recommendations of the majority party and minority groups in the House of Assembly—of the three, two represented the majority party and one the minority groups.

The Executive Council was the policy-making body. It consisted of ten members with the Governor as chairman—six elected ministers, three officials and one member selected by the Upper House. The three officials had between them the most important portfolios—foreign and Commonwealth affairs; defence and police; information and broadcasting, law and order and finance.

From the very outset our party opposed the Waddington Constitution. On the first publication of the Waddington report, in the latter part of 1951, I pointed out at a press conference in London the weaknesses of the Constitution, and exposed the limitations of the various checks and balances which the Commission considered "essential and integral features of democratic government as Western civilisation understands it". Our Constitution had many more checks than balances—it is useful to compare them with those in the United States.

In the U.S. the Senate is elected, not nominated like our State Council which has the power to delay legislation passed by our Lower House for one year. The President of the United States is elected by the people; our Governor receives his appointment from the Queen through the Secretary of State for Colonies. While the veto of the President of the United States can be over-ruled by a two-thirds majority in a joint session of both Houses of Congress, the Governor's veto in British Guiana is absolute.

In addition, the Governor has powers of certification. "In the interests of public faith, public order and good government" not only can he veto Bills passed by the legislature; he can also declare passed any Bills which have been rejected by the legislature. There are also many important subjects—defence, tariffs, external relations and constitutional questions—which are reserved for H.M. Government in Britain.

The checks written into the Waddington Constitution were fundamentally designed to maintain the status quo, to protect the imperialist interests of the British Government with its need for primary products to meet Britain's dollar deficit, and to protect the colony's capitalists and their profits.

This was clearly stated on more than one occasion in the Waddington report. The commission said, for instance:

" . . . if a real measure of economic expansion is to be

achieved, further capital must be attracted from official and private enterprise. If this capital is to be forthcoming nothing must be done which can sap confidence . . . there must be no fear that impulsive action will undermine industry or that ill-considered taxation will deter legitimate investments."

Again according to Sir John Waddington:

" . . . the situation can only be met by an expanding economy which will demand for its fulfilment the investment of considerable capital from overseas and consequently a full measure of confidence in the rule of Government."

In these conditions we felt it would be impossible to make any significant changes in the structure of economic power in the country. We felt that such changes—possibly nationalisation of sugar, land reform, schemes for diversified agriculture and so on—were essential if the conditions of "economic stagnation" described by the Evans Commission of 1948 were not to continue.

We could see no reason why our Constitution should not have been at least as liberal as that of our neighbours in Dutch Guiana. Their Constitution had none of the objectionable features of our own. Their Government is responsible only to the freely elected legislature. There is no nominated Upper House. The Governor does not sit in the Cabinet; and the Executive Council is made up entirely of elected members of the Legislative Council. With the exception of defence and foreign relations, their autonomy is absolute.

Despite our opposition, the Waddington Constitution—I was the only member in the old Council to oppose it—came into force in March 1953, and the first general election to be based on universal adult suffrage took place in April.

Our party had a definite programme. Our policy was straightforward and constitutional. We wanted, like the Labour Party in Britain, to bring a Socialist new deal to the lives of the working people of our country. Here is an outline of the main proposals in our programme:

In the *social sphere,* our programme included a social security scheme ; first steps towards a free health service and workmen's compensation to cover industrial diseases; and speedier implementation of the Factories Ordinance.

In *education* we campaigned for Government-controlled and secular education—252 of the 269 State-aided primary schools are in the hands of one or other of the religious denominations. We accepted religious education in the schools. We wanted more secondary school scholarships, and the provision of more nursery schools.

In *farming* our proposed measures included land reform, land settlement, security of tenure for farmers and provision for agricultural loans. We urged a centrally planned drainage and irrigation system—so as to make available for agriculture large tracts of hitherto uncultivated land—in place of specific schemes mainly designed to benefit the sugar estates.

In *housing* we wanted low-rental building schemes. In *administration* we wanted reform of land government, introduction of universal suffrage, better control of the expenditure of the Public Works Department and an inquiry into its administration.

In *finance* we wanted an increase of direct taxes accompanied by a reduction of indirect taxes.

And in *industry* we wanted the establishment of new industries.

We intended to amend all existing laws and regulations which restricted the civil liberties of the people—such as the banning of books, films and individuals. And we intended to pass laws to protect trade unions, repeal the Trades Disputes (Essential Services) Ordinance, and bring into force a measure for the recognition of trade unions based on the U.S. Wagner Act. All these things were clearly laid down in our election programme as part of our appeal to the people.

During the election a fierce campaign was launched against us by our opponents with the help of the press, pulpit and radio. They devoted most of their attacks to the irrelevant but familiar issues of international plots, forced labour camps, Communism and the Soviet Union. This was to be expected.

In all this the newspapers took a leading part. This was not surprising, for the three daily newspapers—the *Daily*

Chronicle, the *Daily Argosy* and the *Guiana Graphic*—have interlocking directorates representing sugar, mining, commerce and banking.

On the two Sundays before the election all three daily papers circulated a four-page supplement published by the Man-Power Citizens' Association. This was certainly a costly venture, and one wonders how this not very prosperous trade union organisation was able to finance the supplement. Its main attack was on the People's Progressive Party.

In addition to our party, three others fought, besides the many individuals who stood as independents. The main plank of the opposition was hatred of the People's Progressive Party which symbolised the people's movement. Some sections of the opposition had no policy and did not bother to put forward a programme; others borrowed extensively from our programme, but had no intention of carrying out such a policy.

All the other parties were united in their campaign against us ; in this they were also joined by the churches. The usual propaganda was used—that we would confiscate the people's lands, burn down their churches, that the property and savings of people would be taken from them and that even their family rights would be destroyed.

There was also the story that we were being financed by "red gold" from Moscow. But the truth was that we fought the election on a very limited budget—in fact we had to borrow money to put down deposits for some of our candidates. On election day many of our candidates had no loudspeaker equipment, and indeed quite a lot of them had to conduct their campaigns by bicycle or on foot, not being able to afford a car.

It is easy to understand why the churches should support the established order. Many had a vested interest. Some received financial assistance from the planters. Not so long ago, the Anglican Church received $55,000 from Booker's to build a convent. The Portuguese, main pillar of the Catholic Church, were the most reactionary. When the Constitution Commission came to British Guiana, the Portuguese, acting through the Sword of the Spirit, opposed universal adult suffrage.

The elections were very orderly. Indeed, the Commissioner of Police, who had kept the volunteer force as a reserve in case of trouble, said these were among the most orderly elections he had ever seen.

We won eighteen of the twenty-four seats, and the National Democratic Party won two. Four independents were also elected. Most of the six seats which our party did not win were in remote interior districts very costly to organise.

Elected with this absolute majority, we secured the six elected ministries. The Governor assigned portfolios to us on May 28, and after the Coronation celebrations, towards the middle of June, we took office.

While we were in the middle of our new activities—carrying out our legislative duties, getting adjusted to our new surroundings, fulfilling our election pledges—the troops came to British Guiana, and, limited though it was, our Constitution was suspended.

CHAPTER SIX

EXCUSES HAD TO BE FOUND

"Oh, what a tangled web we weave,
When first we practice to deceive."
WALTER SCOTT

So our Constitution was suspended. In our case there was not the familiar dress rehearsal. There was no shooting, no violence, no terrorism. But some excuse had to be given; the bogy of Communism was the most convenient. So there was a "red plot". Nothing original.

Not being able to make any specific charges, the British Government built its case on "ifs" and "buts". The original statement, attempting to justify the despatch of troops and warships, spoke of "intrigues" by "Communists and their associates, some in ministerial posts". But nothing specific.

The statement continued: "If this process were to continue unchecked an attempt might be made by methods which are familiar in other parts of the world to set up a Communist State. This would lead to bloodshed. . . ."

But the "red plot" pill was not easily swallowed. True, the *Daily Express* on October 5 talked in its usual emphatic way of "The first dramatic step to forestall a Communist plot to seize power in the colony of British Guiana and turn it into a Red State". But the more staid press organs asked for greater proof. *The Times* wrote, "Thoughtful observers feel that unless the show of force is justified by the subsequent revelation of an imminent plot, it may well alienate public opinion". The *Observer* of October 11 spoke in strong terms of the Government's "serious blunders" and "serious mistakes".

But the White Paper on the suspension of the Constitution did not supply any further evidence. *The Times* of October 21 commented: "The 'Communist plot' . . . is not exposed in the White Paper with the clarity and completeness that many in the country expected." A few days later, after the debate on British Guiana in the House of Commons, the *Economist* also admitted : "The White Paper has not cleared up many people's doubts."

The main charges in the White Paper fell under three headings.

First, it was said we fomented strikes for political ends and we attempted to oust established trade unions by legislative action.

It is difficult to understand why the charge of fomenting strikes for political purposes was made. For we had obtained a big parliamentary majority that allowed us to carry out our plans without resort to strike action, even if we had wanted such action. We had just come through the April elections with eighteen out of twenty-four seats.

The White Paper alleges that we were attempting by legislative action to crush established trade unions; by this is meant the Man-Power Citizens' Association, which was recognised by the sugar planters as the bargaining agent for the sugar workers. The White Paper quotes the membership of this union as 8,272 against a membership of 817 for the Guiana Industrial Workers' Union, the unrecognised union. The impression created is that we were forcing on the employers a union that had no following.

Our Labour Relations Bill did not say that the G.I.W.U. or any specific union should be recognised by the employers. It empowered the Minister of Labour to authorise a poll in any industry in which there was no recognised union or where a dispute existed between two or more unions for recognition as the bargaining agent. In the former case an employer was forced to recognise any union that secured 51 per cent of the votes at a poll conducted by the Labour Department. But in the latter case where a union was already recognised, the challenging union had to secure at least 65 per cent of the votes. This went beyond the U.S. National Labour Relations Act which stipulated only a bare majority of 51 per cent.

If the figures quoted in the White Paper are correct, then the Man-Power Citizen's Association had nothing to fear. All it had to do was to secure 36 per cent of the votes at any poll.

But the White Paper figures do not tell the true story. They are statistical lies, like so many other lies—and some big plain ones —in the White Paper.

First of all, the M.P.C.A. does not organise only sugar workers. Its membership is spread over many occupations. It is true that the bulk of the members were sugar workers. But we should remember that this union had negotiated with the sugar planters a Provident Scheme (in place of the contributory pensions scheme recommended by the Venn Report, which the planters did not accept on grounds of financial inability). To participate in this scheme workers had to be members of the M.P.C.A. In fact the employers very kindly deducted union dues from the pay envelopes of the workers.

The White Paper gave the Guiana Industrial Workers' Union a membership of 817; but the Colonial Office report for 1950 gave it a membership of 3,000. To understand why this union had suffered a drop in membership, and, indeed, why in 1950 it had only 3,000 members out of a possible total of 30,000 workers in the sugar industry, is to know the conditions prevailing on the sugar estates.

Militant leaders were given trespass notices if they went to the estates. Workers who became members of the G.I.W.U. were often ejected from their homes. In conditions of unemployment and under-employment, fear dominated the workers' lives. The employers always found some pretext for refusing employment to militant trade union leaders. The result was that though many supported this union they did not become actual members.

The election results tell the tale. The M.P.C.A. supported the National Democratic Party at the general election in 1953 ; Mr. Lionel Luckhoo, its president, was also vice-president of the National Democratic Party, and its secretary and vice-president were also candidates of the Party. But when the election results were declared the National Democratic Party had won two seats—and neither was in a "sugar constituency".

The G.I.W.U., on the other hand, supported our Party. Eleven of the twenty-four constituencies in the colony were sugar constituencies—and we won them all with overwhelming majorities.

This could only mean one thing; that the membership figures of the two unions give not the slightest indication of the confidence placed in them by the workers. In fact, in the Berbice

River constituency, where 70-80 per cent of the voters are sugar and bauxite workers, the secretary of the M.P.C.A. not only lost his seat to the vice-president of the G.I.W.U., but even lost his deposit.

In an article in *Tribune* on November 27, 1953, Mr. Ian Mikardo, M.P., wrote about this so-called trade union:

"I have before me as I write, a journal called *The Labour Advocate,* which describes itself as the 'Official organ of the Man-Power Citizens' Association'. It is the issue dated October 18, 1953, and it is the first number published after the suspension of the Constitution of British Guiana.

"The main article in this paper is a straightforward defence of two things—of capitalism in general and colonial employers in particular.

"Nowhere in the paper is there any reference to the low wages and unspeakable living conditions of the workers of British Guiana. To read it you would believe that the members of the Man-Power Citizens' Association enjoy high wages and ideal conditions provided by the most generous and beneficent employers one could imagine.

"Capitalism is described as a 'dynamic, expanding system' and as a 'bold and imaginative society'. The article pays a series of warm tributes to the employers. It even gives them credit for the abolition of slavery (which, in fact, they fiercely opposed), establishing industrial safety (which, in fact, they haven't cared twopence about) and for 'nearly abolishing' woman and child labour (which, in fact, they have struggled to retain).

"But the most interesting feature of the official organ of the Man-Power Citizens' Association is not its editorial matter, but its advertisements.

"In this trade union journal there are 146 column inches of text and ninety-four column inches of employers' advertisements. The back page contains a full-page advertisement for—guess who? You've got it—Booker's. It is pretty obvious where the money comes from to keep this journal going.

"What would any A.E.U. member think if he received his union journal one morning and found 40 per cent of it taken up by advertisements of the Engineering and Allied Employers' National Federation?

"Yet it is this Man-Power Citizens' Association, this obvious goose club, which British trade unionists are being told by their leaders to support."

Other half-page and one-third page advertisements carried by this paper are from other big companies such as Sandbach Parker and Co. (a trading company tied up to the Demerara Co. Ltd.), Sprostons and Co. Ltd. (a sister trading company of Demerara Bauxite Co. Ltd.), Demerara Electric Co. and the Demerara Tobacco Co. (a subsidiary of an American tobacco trust).

Secondly, we were charged with trying to get control of the public services. In British Guiana the most senior positions are, with few exceptions, held by officials usually brought out from the United Kingdom. As part of our wide appeal during the election campaign we said that qualified Guianese should have priority in all appointments.

The senior officials paid lip service to this policy, but opposed it for obvious reasons in private and in practice. Our attitude has been entirely misinterpreted by the White Paper.

It should be remembered that though in Britain the civil servants work with the Government in power, in British Guiana the Governor and the senior civil servants *are* the Government—administering the country for the sugar, mining and commercial interests. Before the election which returned us to office, these officials had always been against us; after the election they were not only placed in the Cabinet, but were put in our ministries. Some worked openly against us. What we attempted was something which the late Professor Laski referred to as "marrying" the good qualities of the permanent civil service system of Britain with the party civil service system of the U.S.A.

Many examples show the subserviency of the official administration to the planters and the vested interests.

For instance, in 1921 the Government bought from the Demerara Railway Company derelict railway stock and assets. Cash payment was not made. The agreement stipulated a payment to the original owners of a *perpetual* annuity of nearly $84,000 a year. This burden we have already carried for more than thirt' years—and it is supposed to last for ever.

Recently the Government acquired from Booker Bros, McConnell and Co. 252 acres of land at Campbellville for $480,000. This is ninety-six times the 1937 purchase price; at that time about 3,000 acres of land were bought for $60,000. Under the agreement then made, debenture bonds were issued by the company, bearing interest rate of 3½ per cent. From this interest alone a revenue of $16,800 a year was obtained for only 252 acres, while the company had never earned in administering the whole estate as much as $10,000 in any one of the three years, 1938, 1939, 1940.

The third major charge in the White Paper was that we were undermining the loyalty of the police, and that by intimidation and force of various kinds we intended to organise a People's Police and set up a "one-party Communist state" in British Guiana.

I am quoted in the White Paper as saying on May 3:

> "Comrades, in the past when we asked for bread we were given bullets, and those who fired at the workers were honoured by our masters. But when the P.P.P. gets into power the same bullets which were fired on those poor people will be fired on our oppressors. We shall organise a police force. It will be known as the People's Police."

In the past the police were used as instruments of oppression against workers. Sugar workers were shot at the plantations of Leonora, Riumveldt and, as recently as 1948, Enmore. The Government Enmore Inquiry Committee set up to inquire into the shooting said:

> "We are, however, of the opinion that the evidence has established that after the first few shots there was firing which went beyond the requirements of the situation, with the results that Pooran, noticeably, and some others, received bullets when in actual flight."

Pooran and four others were killed and others severely injured. But instead of being brought to trial for this, the officer-in-charge was decorated by the Government.

What we wanted was a neutral police to keep normal law and order. Words are put into my mouth when I am alleged to have said: "We shall organise a police force. It will be known as the People's Police." What I in fact said was: "We need a People's Police."

This speech was made after we had won the elections with an overwhelming majority, and when I was fully aware that by our new Constitution the police force was not under the elected Minister but the Chief Secretary. The Governor was commander-in-chief of the armed forces. In these conditions it was, of course, impossible to think of organising a People's Police.

The Minister of Labour, Mr. Ashton Chase, is charged in the White Paper with interfering with the police, and is reported to have said:

> "It is nauseating to find that as soon as there is a labour dispute or stoppage of work—no matter how trivial or large—the police intervene. . . . Any repetition of the past attitude and conduct by the police will meet with stern action on the part of the elected ministers."

Ministers, particularly the Minister of Works and the Minister of Labour, did complain in the Executive Council about the action of the police in labour disputes. On one occasion at Plantation Lusignan, where the Inspector of Labour was interrogating some workers, the police were found taking notes and names of the workers. Undoubtedly these names found their way into the hands of the sugar planters. The Minister of Labour rightly felt that this practice should cease.

Another section of the White Paper deals with the alleged danger of violence in British Guiana. I am again misquoted in support of the allegation. I am accused of making an inflammatory speech on March 10, and I am quoted as saying:

> "In Kenya, the Africans are not only killing white men who take their land, but are killing their own people who turn stooges, and that should be done to stooges (here) . . . who are fighting the cause of the Government and not the people."

In the first place, I did not say "should", but "may be done". This quotation was, of course, lifted out of its context. The speech was meant as advice and warning to those who were bent on taking away more and more of the people's rights. It was made immediately after the old Legislative Council had passed a Bill giving the Governor in Council the power to ban the entry into British Guiana of books, films, gramophone records, and the Postmaster General the right to open private mail.

The civic rights of many persons are severely restricted. For instance, Dr. J. P. Lachhmansingh, president of the Guiana Industrial Workers' Union, was charged on two occasions with trespassing in sugar plantations. A damage suit of £1,000 was filed against me for trespassing in my own constituency! I was declared a "prohibited immigrant" by the Governments of Trinidad and Leeward Islands. So was my wife. As I have already said, prominent Caribbean labour and political leaders were not allowed to enter our country. Books and pamphlets imported by me from the United Kingdom were seized and burned.

The Minister of Education is quoted as having said in the House of Assembly on September 11: "The possibility of our present Constitution being taken from us . . . will be met by as much force as necessary." What was left out of this quotation was "in the circumstances". After the suspension of the Constitution, our resistance was by non-violence and non-co-operation. This speech, be it noted, was made in the House of Assembly to the leader of the Opposition who a few weeks before threatened (apparently he was more informed of the Government's secrets than we) that Her Majesty's Government would suspend our Constitution.

Another speech made at a public meeting on September 24 was credited to the Minister of Education, but actually it was delivered by the Minister of Labour. He is stated to have said:

> "They say they are going to take away the Constitution from us, but I would like them to know that when they attempt that, Her Gracious Majesty will not only hear the explosion of the atomic bomb in the hinterland of Australia; but she will hear it in the mudlands of British Guiana, for we intend to fight to the end. I would like not to discuss our

plans for the intended action which we will take, but will keep it a secret until it becomes necessary to put it into operation."

This, again, was made after rumours that our Constitution would be taken away. What was clearly political rhetoric—as later non-violence showed—has been selected as a serious charge by the Colonial Office.

Arson is also one of the major charges listed in the White Paper. This was given a great deal of publicity by the *Daily Express*. The White Paper says it was established from reliable sources that we planned to set fire to business property and to residences of prominent Europeans and Government officials in Georgetown.

This is indeed a grave charge, and we challenged the Government to arraign us with it before the courts. Asked in the House of Commons why we were not charged, Mr. Oliver Lyttelton, the Colonial Secretary, disclosed that the "reliable sources" were police agents. This alleged incendiary plan of ours was one of the few specific charges in the White Paper. It was a major reason for the suppression of the Constitution and the dismissal of the Ministers.

Yet, in answer to a question by Mr. Fenner Brockway, M.P., in the House of Commons, it was revealed by Mr. Hopkinson that the alleged plan was "made" on October 7, *three days after* the Queen signed the Order-in-Council on September 4. In other words "our plan to burn down Georgetown" was made, according to the British Government, after counter-measures had been taken to prevent the plan. Needless to say, there has not been a single case of incendiarism in Georgetown. Mr. Lyttelton out-Goebbelled Goebbels and Hitler—for they at least burnt down the Reichstag before accusing the Communists.

The White Paper also spoke of "violent intentions" on the part of P.P.P. leaders. It said:

> "On September 24, 1953, . . . large crowds had been instigated by the P.P.P. and the G.I.W.U. leaders to assemble in the vicinity of the Legislative Chamber. While the police were attempting to control them, the Minister of Works exhorted them to rush into the building."

This reference is to the time when the Labour Relations Bill was being debated in the House of Assembly. It is not true to say that the Minister exhorted the crowds to rush the building. The fact is that since the elections in April great political interest had been shown and it had become customary for large numbers of people to attend the meetings of the House. The gallery was very small; before, it had been deserted, now it was always filled to capacity.

The White Paper also spoke of a well-developed cell system organised by the P.P.P. with "a hard core of some 400 to 500 Party members who are ready to do violence at the bidding of the leaders, particularly Mr. King". Note the words "are ready". Not one instance of violence has been cited by the Government. The word "cell" is used to impute some sort of sinister character to the P.P.P., but actually the Party is organised on the same basis as the Labour Party in Britain.

Paragraph 8 of the White Paper dealt with two so-called grave charges—the removal of the ban on the entry of West Indians and the introduction of a Bill to repeal the Undesirable Publications Ordinance, popularly known as the Subversive Literature Bill.

In 1952 six prominent West Indian political and trade union leaders were declared by the Governor of British Guiana "prohibited immigrants" and were not allowed to enter British Guiana. They were:

Richard Hart, former vice-president of the Jamaica Trades Union Congress, and executive committee member of the People's National Party; Ferdinand Smith, representative of the World Federation of Trade Unions and president of the Jamaican Federation of Trade Unions; John La Rose, secretary of the Independence Party of Trinidad and Tobago; Quentin O'Connor, secretary of the Cosmopolitan Workers' Trade Union and secretary of the Trinidad T.U.C.; John Rojas, president of the Oilfield Workers' Union, which is the largest union in Trinidad, and president also of the Trinidad T.U.C.; and Billy Strachan, secretary of the Caribbean Labour Congress London Branch.

Flight-Lieutenant Strachan volunteered during the war and served with an R.A.F. bomber squadron; he was severely injured while flying over Germany. He wanted to preserve the world for democracy and the Four Freedoms!

The P.P.P. believes in the freedom of movement of all peoples in British Guiana, especially West Indians. Indeed, the second point in our programme is Federation of Guiana and the West Indies, with full internal self-government for each unit. We do not see any reason why our doors, which were open to imperialist robbers, should be closed to West Indian patriots, whether they believe in Communism or any other political creed.

These bans were contrary to the principles laid down in the Universal Declaration of Human Rights regarding free movement of individuals.

We make no apology for seeking to repeal a law which gives the Government power to prohibit literature and films and to open private mail. Of course we sought to repeal such a law; anybody who prizes freedom would support such an action.

It was in March 1953 that the former Legislative Council hastily rushed through a Bill giving the Governor power to decide what books, films and gramophone records should be allowed to enter the country. A few months before that the Governor had confiscated several bundles of books imported from the United Kingdom and destroyed them by burning. This is contrary to Article 9 of the Universal Declaration of Human Rights, which says:

> "Everyone has the right of freedom of opinion and expression. This includes freedom to hold opinions without interference, to seek, and to receive information and ideas through any media and regardless of frontiers."

These same rights were supposed to apply to us when the British Government ratified at the Council of Europe the Convention on Human Rights.

The Archbishop of the West Indies, who is also the Archbishop of British Guiana, is not a friend of the P.P.P., and his support was claimed by Lyttelton in the House of Commons debate on British Guiana. But here is something the Archbishop said as a member of the State Council during the Council's debate on the motion to repeal the Undesirable Publications Ordinance:

"I thought then, and I still think, the Ordinance was ineffective, ill-timed, undesirable and entirely mischievous. . . . With all my heart I have revolted against this Ordinance ever since it was first put out in the form of a Bill, and I am only thankful for this opportunity to say something to support its repeal. This is an infringement of the liberty of the individual. That is not just restraint. If absolute freedom is licence, then this is absolute tyranny. . . .

"I am pleased this afternoon to have the opportunity warmly to support the motion that this detestable Ordinance should be repealed and taken, once and for all, off the Statute Books of this Colony, and, I hope, never to return thereto."

There is much talk in the White Paper about our ties with international Communist organisations. Certainly some leaders of the P.P.P. went to Eastern Europe or attended conferences there. Is this an offence? If it is, things have come to a pretty pass, and freedom has been lost on the way. And of course many prominent people from Britain—Members of Parliament, businessmen, clergymen—have been to Eastern Europe. Do they apologise for their visits? Of course not. Why should they? And neither do we apologise.

The P.P.P. is a broad alliance of all progressive forces that are struggling for the freedom and independence of British Guiana, and the social and economic well-being of its inhabitants. It does not question, as do some other nationalist parties, the ideologies of its members, so long as they remain loyal to the Party's programme. Nor should it question them. In this it certainly shows a more tolerant and civilised attitude than the Governor and his friends.

Reference is made in the White Paper to the visit of Mr. Sydney King and Mr. R. O. Westmaas to the World Peace Congress. The P.P.P. does not regard membership of the World Peace Movement as a Communist monopoly; many non-Communists the world over belong to this organisation.

As Colonials, we realise that unless new development schemes are embarked upon our standard of living will continue to be very low. Vast sums of money are being spent on armaments and war preparations. If only a fraction of this wealth could be used for construction projects in backward territories like British Guiana, the lives of the people there could quickly be changed.

We see nothing wrong with the Peace Appeal of the last World Peace Congress, which said:

> "A great hope has been born. Everybody now sees that agreement is possible. The slaughter can be ended. The Cold War can be stopped.
>
> "In this hour we solemnly call upon the peoples to demand of their Governments that they negotiate and agree.
>
> "It is for us to support every move—from whatsoever government it may come—to solve disputes by peaceful means. It is for us all to frustrate the efforts of those who prevent or delay agreement.
>
> "Peace is within our reach. It is for us to win it."

I am listed as having attended the World Youth Festival at Berlin in 1951. This was known to the Colonial Office on my return to London; yet I was taken by them to Scotland on a conducted tour. No mention is made of this in the White Paper, naturally. At that time the hope was perhaps entertained that I too, like many other Colonial "politicians", had my price.

Finally there was the charge, apparently made quite seriously, that we sought to undermine the position and influence of the Boy Scouts and the Girl Guides!

We wanted to change the blatant bias shown by school text books which spoke of the glories of the British Empire and referred to Clive and Warren Hastings as great patriots. This was evidence of our Communist intentions—if this is what the Communists want they have the agreement of all truly democratic people. So also was interpreted the fact that we wanted to abolish the class control of schools through the Church and the Government. This, incidentally, was a recommendation made many years ago by the Colonial Development and Welfare Education Officer to the West Indies.

Perhaps one may sum up the White Paper in the words of the *New Statesman and Nation* on October 24:

> "Most of the White Paper, indeed, may be disposed of by one or two comments. Where there is evidence of conspiracy

or incitement to violence, there could and should have been criminal proceedings which would have tested the evidence in public. Where the allegations are merely of incompetence or of 'evil communications', the proper answer was made by Creech Jones in this journal last week. It is that at a certain stage of colonial development there is no satisfactory alternative to the risks, very real though they are, involved in giving self-government."

CHAPTER SEVEN

WORDS AND FACTS

"Although you come in thousands from the sea,
Although you walk, like locusts, in the street,
Although you point your guns straight at my heart,
I clench my fist above my head,
I sing my song of Freedom."

MARTIN CARTER

"Today when the call of independence is given in the streets, voices without number answer in response. In ten days and less, the whole nation vibrates with its echo, and even the women and children vie with each other with no fear in their hearts. . . . Though you cut down and kill those who rise up everywhere you may change the face of things, but the heart of it, never. Every man has written in his soul the word Independence, and those who in the quiet of their rooms shout for it are beyond the possibility of numbering. Will you arrest and kill them all?"

KIM YUN SIK and YI YONG CHIK

The appointed day was October 22. The great debate on British Guiana had begun. I looked down on Her Majesty's Government and Opposition from the gallery.

The ground had been well prepared for Mr. Lyttelton by the national Press. With the exception of the *Daily Worker* (which said, "Now it's war against British Guiana"), the national dailies printed sensational headlines. Here are some. *Daily Mirror,* October 5: "JANET BRITAIN-HATER—HATRED OF BRITAIN IS MAINSPRING THAT MAKES MRS. JAGAN TICK." *Daily Mail,* October 7: "PLOT TO SEIZE BRITISH GUIANA. NAVY SPEEDING TROOPS." *News Chronicle,* October 7: "GUIANA PLOT EXPOSED. ARMED FORCES SENT TO AVERT RED-STYLE COUP". *Daily Express,* October 6: "BRITISH HOMES STACK GUNS. GOVERNOR BOOED. MOBS STONE CHIEF ANTI-COMMUNIST M.P. WIVES TOLD, QUIT PLANTATIONS."

On the day before the debate the headlines were even more sensational. On October 21 the *Daily Herald* said: "JAGAN

MEN HAD PLOT TO SET CAPITAL ON FIRE". *Daily Express*: "JAGANS APED MAU TERROR." *Daily Mail*. "GUIANA FIRE-BUG PLOT EXPOSED."

Mr. Lyttelton was in good debating form. But he read from a carefully prepared speech. He began by shedding crocodile tears. To suspend the Constitution was a great set-back; for after all, it was still "our national policy" to give "the people in the colonial territories an increasing responsibility in management of their own affairs". But Jagan and company were such bad people. They had come to England to appeal for help, but the Opposition must be on guard, for these people had no friends anywhere—not even in their own country or in their neighbouring West Indies. Then he read out some names and telegrams. He cited Guianese organisations, the League of Coloured Peoples and the British Guiana Village Chairman's Conference, who supported the British intervention.

No doubt Mr. Lyttelton thought he was on safe ground here: the Opposition would not know what these organisations really were, and Mr. Burnham and I could only listen from the gallery.

But the fact is that both these bodies have gone on record very recently against universal adult suffrage.

The Village Chairman's Conference represents unions of local authorities—that is, regional rural areas which embrace two types of authority, village councils and country districts. Village councils have in addition to elected members (chosen on a restricted franchise) one-third of their members nominated. Members of country districts are all nominated. There are about twice as many country districts as village councils. The chairmen of all these bodies form the Village Chairman's Conference, and needless to say they opposed our local government reform which sought to grant universal suffrage, abolish nominated seats and elevate country districts to village status.

The League of Coloured Peoples is not, like the League of Coloured Peoples in Britain, an organisation representing all coloured peoples. In Guiana it is a racialist African organisation. At one time it was very powerful in the city of Georgetown, but it has lost its grip among its followers because of its reactionary role. Its vice-president, Dr. J. Nicholson, and its secretary,

Mr. John Carter, who were elected members in the Legislative Council, 1948-1953, lost their seats at the 1953 elections. Dr. Nicholson soon after the 1947 elections became a good and staunch Government supporter. He refused to read out in the Legislative Council a statement criticising the Budget speech of the Financial Treasurer. Outside the House he agreed to oppose many of the tax proposals in the Budget, but when the time came to vote in the Legislature he supported them. Since the advent of the People's Progressive Party in January 1950 the League of Coloured Peoples has lost support, particularly in Georgetown which was its stronghold.

Both these organisations were on the point of being eclipsed. Their approval of the landing of British troops can be understood—they had a vested interest.

Mr. Lyttelton then quoted opposition to the P.P.P. from Mr. Norman Manley, of the People's National Party, and Mr. Grantley Adams, a well-known figure in Barbados. Of these two I shall have more to say. Then, after mentioning that notorious demagogue, Mr. Bustamente, Chief Minister of Jamaica, he moved on to Dr. Rita Hinden, one of the colonial theoreticians of the Labour Opposition in Britain.

Mr. Lyttelton quoted Dr. Hinden to the effect that on her visit to British Guiana as a member of the Waddington Constitution Commission she gathered that our interpretation of democracy was what she "could only describe as one-party rule".

History is moving too fast for people like Dr. Hinden. She wrote some good books on the colonial question before the Labour Government took office in 1945. It was her own words we quoted in support of our constitutional demands when the Commission took evidence in Guiana. I suppose Dr. Hinden will never recover from the booing she received in London in 1951; perhaps it was the first time she had been booed by colonials. The occasion was a meeting in October 1951 under the joint auspices of the League of Coloured Peoples and the Caribbean Labour Congress, at which both she and I spoke on the British Guiana Constitution.

The Commons debate was notable for the fact that with the

exception of one or two Labour back benchers the Opposition was not prepared to do real battle. Mr. Attlee and Mr. Griffiths were the principal Opposition speakers. Many of the members of the left wing of the Labour Party who were prepared to speak strongly could not catch the Speaker's eye.

Mr. Griffiths spent most of his time admonishing us and saying we had missed a glorious opportunity. It appeared that the right wing, which controlled the Party, had fallen completely for the line used by Mr. Lyttelton. His tactics were clever. He delved into the Opposition's armoury and chose their special weapon—anti-Communism. He quoted from their friends and from their newspaper.

What the *Tribune* called a "tepid amendment" was tabled by the Opposition. It said that the House : "While emphatically deploring the actions and speeches of some of the leaders of the People's Progressive Party in British Guiana, as set forth in the White Paper, and condemning methods tending to the establishment of a totalitarian régime in a British Colony, nevertheless is not satisfied that the situation in British Guiana was of such a character as to justify the extreme step of suspending the Constitution."

When put to the vote this was lost with 256 votes for and 294 against; Mr. Lyttelton's tactics had won the day.

That the Opposition was not prepared to make British Guiana a fighting national issue became clear in the weeks following the debate. Hardly two weeks had passed when the Trades Union Congress issued a strong statement against us. It criticised us for pursuing a Communist policy and maintaining "contacts behind the Iron Curtain, with the World Federation of Trade Unions rather than the Trades Union Congress and the International Confederation of Trade Unions." It added that "to this end the People's Progressive Party through its Ministers had also consistently endeavoured to destroy the Man-Power Citizens' Association, the only existing trade union organisation with collective bargaining agreements, and which provides for the establishment of joint negotiating machinery, which has resulted in a considerable improvement in the conditions of sugar workers."

The statement continued: "Failing by strikes and intimidation to gain its end, i.e. the recognition of the Guiana Industrial Workers' Union, the People's Progressive Party sought to accomplish their aim by legislative action, which would have placed in the hands of Ministers—who at the same time were leaders of unions in opposition to the Man-Power Citizens' Association, which is affiliated to the I.C.F.T.U.—powers which would have enabled them to achieve their industrial objective and at the same time ensure the subservience of the trade union movement to the People's Progressive Party."

Our greatest crime, apparently, was that we did not support the M.P.C.A. which the British T.U.C. was supporting through the International Confederation of Trade Unions. I have already fully described the position of the M.P.C.A. and the G.I.W.U.

This position had apparently not yet dawned on the T.U.C. But surely affiliation to the I.C.F.T.U. should not be the only criterion for help and support. I know the I.C.F.T.U. is in many ways the apple of the T.U.C.'s eye. But more important to me was the unity of our national movement and the success of our struggles for freedom and bread.

I say frankly that with the formation of the I.C.F.T.U., disunity instead of unity emerged on every front in the Caribbean.

Let us go back a few years. In 1945 there was held in Paris a founding conference out of which was formed the World Federation of Trade Unions. To this conference went many representatives from the Caribbean area with the blessings of the British Government and the British T.U.C. In the same year a West Indian conference in British Guiana laid the basis for the Caribbean Labour Congress which united all progressive trade unions and political parties in the Caribbean. Grantley Adams became president, Richard Hart, secretary, Norman Manley, of Jamaica, and H. N. Critchlow, of British Guiana, vice-presidents.

In the immediate post-war period there began a movement of the peoples in the colonial countries for political and economic freedom. In the Far East, in Malaya, pressing demands were being put forward for independence. In the African colonies—Nigeria and the Gold Coast particularly—the people were on the march. Important constitutional demands were made by us in the Caribbean. In face of these demands and the unity of the trade union and political movement in the backward colonial and semi-colonial countries, the imperialist powers began to stiffen their resistance.

It was in this period that the split came about in the World Federation of Trade Unions. The International Confederation of Trade Unions was formed, and this split in the international trade union movement became reflected in the Caribbean Labour scene. Mr. Grantley Adams, Mr. Critchlow and Mr. Bradshaw attended the convening conference of the I.C.F.T.U. Thereafter a regional organisation for Latin America was formed, and Mr. Grantley Adams became chairman of the British Caribbean section of this organisation.

Splits followed all over the West Indies. The British Guiana T.U.C. maintained a loose connection with the W.F.T.U., though the British Guiana Labour Union, headed by Mr. Critchlow, became affiliated to the I.C.F.T.U. The Man-Power Citizens' Association also became a strong pillar of the I.C.F.T.U.

In mid-1951, the British Guiana T.U.C. wrote to the I.C.F.T.U. seeking affiliation. This, however, was not immediately granted; more information was requested by the secretariat of the I.C.F.T.U.

During 1952, in the midst of this growing disunity, two significant events occurred.

First, the Man-Power Citizens' Association resigned from the British Guiana T.U.C. This was a result of two resolutions passed by the T.U.C., one asking the Government to enact legislation similar to our Trade Union Relations Bill, described already; the other opposing the Subversive Literature motion, which I have also described, introduced by Mr. Lionel Luckhoo.

Up to 1950, the Man-Power Citizens' Association had successfully resisted the affiliation of the British Guiana Industrial Workers' Union to the British Guiana T.U.C. In mid-1952, however, the president of the Industrial Workers' Union met leaders of the I.C.F.T.U. in Trinidad and Barbados.

He was promised help by these individuals for the recognition of the union. But later that year, Mr. S. Romualdi, the regional director, visited British Guiana, being met at the airport by the secretary of the Man-Power Citizens' Association. He refused to meet the T.U.C. and on departure said the T.U.C. had become "Communist-dominated". Consequently, neither the T.U.C. nor the Guiana Industrial Workers' Union pursued their intention to affiliate with the I.C.F.T.U.

The other significant fact in 1952 was the expulsion, in Jamaica, from the People's National Party of Richard Hart, Arthur Henry, Frank Hill and Ken Hill, allegedly for being Communists. Pressure was exerted on Norman Manley by the right wing for the expulsion of the left wing. This was caused by unavoidable conflicts within the People's National Party. In the right wing of the P.N.P. were many employers and commission agents—the former P.N.P. Mayor, Mr. Seivright, of Kingston, owns a chain of bakeries. The bakery workers were organised in the T.U.C. Another prominent right wing leader, Wills Isaacs, was a commission agent who obtained his orders from big firms whose employees were also organised by the T.U.C.

Towards the middle of 1952, Grantley Adams declared the Caribbean Labour Congress should be disbanded. This development was quite alarming to many of us in the Caribbean; for the C.L.C. was the only unifying body in the whole progressive West Indian movement.

We decided to meet in October, 1952. (This meeting also is listed in the White Paper as being one of sinister intentions.) John La Rose, Rojas and Quintin O'Connor came from Trinidad, R. Hart from Jamaica and E. Joshua from St. Vincent. Our purpose was quite clear. We decided that since national and trade union affiliations, some to the I.C.F.T.U. and others to the W.F.T.U., were disrupting the Caribbean Labour Congress, then the Congress should only affiliate political organisations and that a separate Caribbean Federation of Labour should be formed to bring together all trade unions, free from the entanglements of the I.C.F.T.U. and the W.F.T.U.

This proposition was put to Mr. Adams. Mr. Hart had also brought a message from Ferdinand Smith, representative of the W.F.T.U. in Jamaica, that he would be prepared to recommend financial and other support to such a Caribbean Federation of Labour provided the I.C.F.T.U. would do the same. Mr. Adams would not support such a proposition for unity. He was ready to "bust up" the C.L.C. and the unity of the Labour movement.

Mr. Lyttelton, knowing that Manley and Adams were ideological brothers of the British T.U.C. leaders, quoted their statements in the House of Commons. But it is they, not we, who have changed. The activities of the Caribbean Labour Congress were proving too embarrassing for these so-called leaders. At the 1947 Conference of the C.L.C., at Montego Bay, they had said they were willing to put forward a united militant demand on behalf of the Caribbean peoples for freedom and self-government, and that they were ready to join a Federation of British Colonial Territories only on the ground of dominion status for the Federation and internal self-government for the various unions.

But much water has flowed under the bridge since then. The retreat started in 1948 when Mr. Adams was appointed a delegate to the United Nations Assembly in Paris. He put up a good defence for British imperialism, and for this he was roundly criticised in the colonies. For instance, the *West African Pilot* wrote in October 1948 a caustic editorial:

> ". . . When a . . . group of black men join hands together in order to see to it that a new day dawns for all men of our colour, there is always a willing Negro to join the forces of the enemy. Our readers . . . should mark and digest the news published . . . about the activities of one Mr. G. Adams, of Barbados, in the U.N. sitting in France, and judge for themselves the type of African 'leader' that Britain loves to advertise to the world . . . it is most distressing to note Mr. Adams' every word.
>
> "But we in this part of the world should not have been bothered had Mr. Adams not, without consulting us, without even knowing Africa, gone to array his sentiments before the U.N.
>
> "We have never said that the British are not any good at all: no Negro of worth has even said that. But Mr. Adams ought to have known that the over-all policy of the

Colonial Office stands condemned before all men of good will.

"Mr. Adams, by his irresponsible and inspired utterances, . . . has dealt a wicked blow to all suffering peoples. We can assure him that neither history nor African conscience will be kind to him, when, at long last, the black men of the world come to their own."

But Mr. Adams was highly rewarded—the title of C.M.G. was conferred on him by the reigning monarch.

By 1952, Mr. Adams was no longer talking about Federation with dominion status; he was content to accept colonial status.

The Labour Party statement, which came later, said that "instead of pursuing a policy of social reform and seeking to justify the faith placed in them by the electorate, the leaders of the P.P.P. pursued a Communist policy and created a situation which necessitated the movement of troops to ensure the maintenance of law and order."

The fact is that our election programme and the Bills we had introduced or were about to introduce, were mild reforms, many of which came from either the United Kingdom or the United States, or were adopted in other countries.

Responsible journals in Britain and elsewhere blasted Mr. Lyttelton's phoney "red plot".

For instance the *Times of India* remarked: "In its laboriously prepared charge sheet the British Government has not been able to point to a single act of violence on the part of any member of the People's Progressive Party. . . . The people of this country who remember how, not long ago, the leaders of the national movement were denounced by the British Government as Japanese agents, know what to make of these charges."

CHAPTER EIGHT

WHAT WE WERE DOING

"I go like you to keep faith with the living."
PETER BLACKMAN

A great deal was said by the British Government and the right-wing newspapers about what the People's Progressive Party is and what it intended to do in British Guiana. Most of this has been ignorant surmise, unmitigated slander or sheer malicious lying for political ends.

But the facts are what must count in the eyes of any unprejudiced and normally intelligent person. Let us, therefore, look briefly at what the People's Progressive Party really did during its short term of office.

We passed through the House of Assembly a Bill seeking the repeal of the Undesirable Publications Bill. We removed the ban on the entry of West Indians. These were part of our election manifesto.

The House of Assembly also passed an amendment to the Rice Farmers (Security of Tenure) Bill, 1945, to help rice farmers during a drought. The Bill sought to protect and secure the rights of tenant rice farmers. The 1945 Ordinance, in addition to controlling the rentals of rice lands, placed penalties on landlords and tenants who did not observe the rules of good estate management and good husbandry. The penalty imposed on the tenant if he did not cultivate his land properly was ejection from his holding. But for a landlord who did not keep drains and trenches clean and free from weeds, and dams free from bush, the penalty was that the tenant could vacate the land! This was certainly not much of a penalty for the landlord. Our amendment sought to empower the Government District Commissioner to give the landlord a specified time to undertake the work he was supposed to do by law. If he refused, then the work was to be done by the Government officer at Government expense and the cost was to be recovered from the landlord.

This Bill was described by Mr. Lionel Luckhoo in the State Council as totalitarian dictatorship, and was rejected.

On the day when British troops entered Guiana we passed in the House of Assembly our Labour Relations Bill. Employers were to be made by law to negotiate with trade unions, and to recognise for collective bargaining only unions enjoying majority support.

We campaigned to remove church control of the schools. In British Guiana there is what is popularly known as dual control of the schools. Nearly 95 per cent of the schools are under control of the church. By church, it must be understood is meant the Christian denominations. But in British Guiana nearly one-half of the population is non-Christian. Yet these people are forced to receive Christian religious instruction in the schools. In fact many teachers are forced to become Christians in order to obtain jobs.

Our proposal was merely to have schools under direct supervision of the Government and the local education committees. We did not propose that there should not be religious instruction. We planned to set aside certain periods of the day when any denomination would be allowed facilities to carry on religious teaching.

This was more democratic than the present practice where even other Christian denominations are not allowed to give religious instruction in the same school.

We tightened up on public works expenditure by the Public Works Department—commonly known as the "Public Waste Department". We intended to bring the Public Works Union to play a more effective part in the economical administration of the department. In most instances, the public works expenditure on any construction was generally one-third or one-half greater than would have been incurred by private individuals undertaking the same work.

We initiated legislation to reform local government. We wanted universal adult suffrage, abolition of nominated seats and elevation of nominated country districts to village status. Although universal adult suffrage was granted for the election of members to the House of Assembly, this was not in force for local affairs. The right to vote was still restricted by the ownership of property, and in Georgetown and New Amsterdam by a rental qualification as an alternative.

Although the British Guiana system of local government was highly praised by the Colonial Office and proclaimed a model for colonial territories, it left much to be desired. Local government is divided into four sections—municipalities, village councils, country districts and rural districts. The municipality of Georgetown had nine elected members and three nominated. In the village districts, one-third of the members were nominated, but the bulk of the rural areas were either country districts or rural districts. In the country districts all members were nominated, while the rural districts were under the direct supervision of the Local Government Board. Nominations were, of course, made by the Local Government Board. Actually, it made no difference because all members of the Local Government Board were nominated by the Governor.

We introduced legislation to suspend the Essential Services Act, which was a temporary war-time measure, and were drafting plans for a National Labour Board to provide for compulsory arbitration.

We also set up committees to investigate the domestic workers' problem, the revision of the Workmen's Compensation Ordinance and machine pools for farmers.

We appointed ordinary people to Government boards and committees.

To help the poor, we began a revision of the fees of Government doctors. We advocated jobs for local men in the police force and in other categories.

We refused to grant leases of Crown lands to landlords already possessing large holdings.

We intended to increase the rates of mining companies which were paying very nominal rentals. We intended to enact a Land Law and to set up a Land Authority to examine the question of the beneficial utilisation of lands and the development of lands generally. We curtailed unnecessary expenditure of public funds. We refused payment to members of the State Council;

this was in conformity with the recommendations of the Constitution Commission, but contrary to the views of the late Governor, who recommended payment.

We did not think it necessary to send delegates to meet the Queen in Jamaica. Two delegates and their wives were sent to the Coronation celebrations in London. We had already incurred a Coronation expenditure of $100,000.

We cut out extravagant house-building for senior Government officials. A few months before the election a public scandal was created when the Government spent more than $96,000 to build four houses for senior civil servants. The Minister of Works also clashed with the manager of the Transport and Harbour Department who was building a luxurious house for himself.

We increased the number of scholarships known as People's Scholarships. There are no university facilities of any kind in British Guiana, and the Government had provided just two scholarships every year for university training—one for boys and one for girls.

A month before the suspension of the Constitution I went to Surinam to secure rights for the Guianese fishermen in Dutch Guiana waters.

In January 1953, three taxes on the sugar planters had been repealed—excise, sugar duty and acreage. These we sought to reimpose.

* * *

Look again at this programme. Is it not the kind of programme for which any progressive person in Britain would give his vote? Does it indicate bloodshed, arson, totalitarian rule? Or does it indicate a desire to help people who sorely need help?

Some of its provisions have origins in the most "respectable" of countries. Our local government reforms came from the United Kingdom, our Labour Relations Bill from the U.S.A., our land law from Puerto Rico, an American colony. It is not surprising that a responsible journal like the *Nation* could remark (November 28, 1953):

> "The measures planned were not Socialist, let alone Communist, in essence. Its planned labour legislation was derived from the Wagner Act. Under the system to be set

up, inquiries and polls could be held in any industry to decide on the union to be officially recognised. The enquiries and polls were to be conducted by a British official.

"What is more, a new union challenging the position of an established bargaining agent would have to get 65 per cent of the workers' votes before it could be recognised.

"It was under these conditions that the P.P.P.-supported union, the Guiana Industrial Workers' Union, hoped to replace the existing Man-Power Citizens' Association as the official organisation in sugar and elsewhere."

What, then, is responsible for the statement of the Labour Party National Executive? Is it because that executive is dominated by T.U.C. leaders who had already issued a strong statement against us for daring to oppose the Man-Power Citizens' Association? Or is it because we had dared to oppose and sometimes strongly criticise the Labour Government during its term of office?

This brings me to another matter—the policy of the Labour Government towards colonial peoples. This is worth some examination.

CHAPTER NINE

LABOUR AND THE COLONIES

"Modern imperialism is in fact to socialists simply capitalism in its most predatory and militant phase."

KEIR HARDIE

"We are great friends of the jolly old Empire and are going to stick to it."

HERBERT MORRISON

Were we wrong to criticise the Labour Government's attitude toward the colonies? The Labour movement must judge us as colonials—it must put itself in our position. Then it may begin to see flaws in the Labour Government's colonial policy.

The late Mr. Ernest Bevin said in the House of Commons in 1946:

> "I know that if the British Empire fell, it would mean the standard of life of our constituents would fall considerably."

Any member of the Labour Party must surely realise the implications of such a statement. If it were true, it would mean that a high standard in Britain could only be based on a low standard of living in the colonies—on the exploitation of the colonial people. In fact, on the exploitation of people like those in British Guiana. And I am sure that no sincere member of the Labour Party could be in favour of such a state of affairs.

To us it sounded like the same old tale. It appeared no different from what Winston Churchill, the arch-imperialist, had said in 1929, when, as Chancellor of the Exchequer, he observed:

> "The income which we derive from commissions and services rendered to foreign countries is over £65 million. In addition we have a steady revenue from foreign investments of close on £300 million a year. This is the explanation of the source from which we are able to defray social services at a level incomparably higher than that of any European country, or any country."

In 1947, during the period of the Labour Government, Mr.

F. J. Seaford, a director of Booker's, was defeated at the elections, but immediately nominated to the Legislative and Executive Councils by the Governor. We protested to the Secretary for the Colonies in Britain—and were informed that it was done in the best interests of the people of the colony.

In 1948 when workers were shot down by the police at Plantation Enmore, the Governor appointed a commission of inquiry. The commission admitted that there was "firing which went beyond the actual needs of the situation". We asked that the police officer in charge be brought to trial. But instead he was decorated.

Throughout the whole term of the Labour Government we saw, coming year after year, the same type of civil servants and governors who had always been sent to the Caribbean, with the single exception of the Socialist Lord Baldwin. The civil servants coming to the West Indies were conservative-minded; they always ruled in a way that was in the interests of the planters. The role of the official was clearly emphasised by Professor Arthur Lewis, who wrote in his booklet, *Labour in the West Indies*:

> "The impression is now widespread among the people that the Governor and officials are little more than tools of the white oligarchy of planters, merchants and bankers in whose society they spend most of their time, and whose will is that the policy of the Government is the policy of the local club, which is decided perhaps over a round of golf or a whisky and soda."

In 1950 the composition of the Constitution Commission which came to British Guiana was tipped in favour of the Tories. Conservative Sir John Waddington, former acting Governor of British Guiana, was chairman. Another member was a Liberal Professor, Vincent Harlow. Dr. Rita Hinden, a Fabian Socialist, who recently joined in the attack against our Party and Government, was the third member.

Mr. James Griffiths, the Labour Colonial Secretary, also alarmed us—to an even greater extent than the Constitution Commission. For while the Commission recommended that only the twenty-four elected members of the Lower House of

Assembly should select the six elected Ministers (thus necessitating a majority of thirteen), Mr. Griffiths recommended that the three official members should also participate in the voting. This would have necessitated a majority not of thirteen but at least fourteen to withstand the opposition, if, with the help of the three officials, it had intended to raid the majority party and win over one or two members with the offer of ministerial posts.

Mr. Griffiths suggested that instead of six elected Ministers in the ten-member Executive Council, there should only be five. This would have meant that the elected would have a 5-4 majority instead of a 6-4 majority. The Governor's position was not clear; for the Constitution Commission's report did not say whether the Governor would have in addition to his casting vote an original vote in the Executive Council. A position of 5-4 majority in favour of the elected, with the Governor holding an original and casting vote, was nothing to be cherished. Then power in the Executive Council would have reposed in the hands of the Governor.

Fortunately for us, the late Governor, Sir Charles Woolley, did not agree with Mr. Griffiths' recommendation. At that time it was expected that we would win five, or, at most, seven seats. And in the change over from the Labour to the Conservative Government, Mr. Lyttelton accepted the views of the Governor.

Let us look at Labour's economic policy towards the colonies. In the King's Speech of March 1950 we are told:

> "My Government is actively promoting the economic and social development of the colonial territories, and the Colonial Development Corporation is proving a useful instrument to this end."

In 1951 Sir Charles Woolley, replying to my criticisms about exploitation in the colonies, almost paraphrased the King's Speech:

> "The primary objective of H.M. Government's declared economic policy towards all its dependent territories—and it is reflected in the establishment of the Colonial Development Corporation—is the development of these territories for the benefit of the people inhabiting them : let there be

no mistake about that. To characterise that policy as imperialist and capitalist exploitation, as has been done in certain quarters, is not only wholly untrue, but mischievous."

But Lord Trefgarne, chairman of the Colonial Development Corporation, addressing a group of Liverpool business men, exploded this myth when he said in 1950:

> "The United Kingdom has an annual dollar deficit of £500 million—that is the background against which the productivity of colonial territories must be viewed. If the Colonies could raise their overall productivity during the next ten years by £200 million a year, that indeed would be a mercy twice blessed.
>
> "The reason why we look to the colonies is that their products, food and raw materials, are more acceptable to the United States than manufactured goods. The total value of imports of manufactured goods into the United States in 1947 from all sources amounted to £250 million. The total imports of food and raw materials were more than four times as great: thanks to tin, rubber, cocoa, etc., the colonial territories overall are playing a good part in the dollar-sterling balance. Obviously, therefore, it is sound policy to aim at greatly increased dollar exports of colonial products."

Little wonder that the Colonial Development Corporation has invested in British Guiana in the extraction of timber and gold. Nearly $2 million have been invested with the British Guiana Consolidated Goldfields Ltd. Gold is necessary to earn dollars.

Industries such as paper, wood pulp, veneer, plywood, glass, cement, electro-cast blocks, which were comprehensively investigated at great expense and recommended by the late consulting engineer, C. O. Chase, and other experts, were not touched.

This same point of view was expressed by Mr. John Strachey, Labour Minister of Food. He put it a little more bluntly:

> "Our national position is really too grave to warrant any indulgence in our particular opinions on the methods of overseas development. By one means or another, by hook or by crook, the development of primary production of all sorts in the colonial territories and dependent areas in the

> Commonwealth in far more abundant quantities than exist today, is, it is hardly too much to say, a matter of life or death for the economy of this country."

"Development" was to take place—but chiefly in a non-industrial direction. The late Sir Stafford Cripps, Labour Chancellor of the Exchequer, underlined this when he addressed in 1947 the African Governors' Conference:

> "You will, I understand, be considering the question of the development of manufactories and industries in the colonies. Though I take the view that such development is highly desirable so long as it is not pushed too far or too quickly, yet it must be obvious that with the present world shortage of capital goods, it is not possible to contemplate much in the way of industrial development of the colonies."

This type of planning was cleary revealed in the Ten-Year Development Plans of colonial territories. It is estimated that of a total contemplated expenditure of £199,422,000 for all the British colonial teritories, £3,356,000 or less than 2 per cent was set aside for industrial electricity and power schemes.

This exploitation of the colonies for dollar purposes was, of course, continued by the Tory Government. The Tory Press was jubilant on the appointment of Mr. Oliver Lyttelton as Secretary for the Colonies in 1951. By this time Britain's dollar balance was worsening. Colonial exploitation was increased.

The Times of November 3, 1951, wrote that the colonies' surplus in dollar trade, which was around $150 million in 1945-49, had risen to $376 million in 1950 and was already $314 million for the first half of 1951. The sterling balances held by the colonies had risen from £510 million in 1947 to £908 million in June 1951.

Malayan tin and rubber were earning in 1951 more dollars than all British exports. British Guiana bauxite not only made strategic aluminium, but also earned dollars. We were allowed to spend only about half our dollar earnings. But still the dollar gap was not closed.

* * *

The statement of the National Executive of the Labour Party said that because of the policy we pursued, the movement of troops became necessary to preserve law and order. There was really no disturbance. I have already alluded to the views of newspaper correspondents who came to Guiana. Consider in addition what the *Daily Mail* reported on October 7:

> "Mr. Whittingham, the deputy police commissioner in British Guiana, sounded calm and unperturbed today as he spoke over the radio-telephone from the colony's capital, Georgetown, and said:
>
> " 'There are no demonstrations, there is no general strike, there is nothing abnormal happening here whatsoever'.
>
> "I told him of reports that Communist workers were demonstrating around the Parliament buildings in Georgetown.
>
> "Mr. Whittingham said: 'There have been no demonstrations and no trouble whatsoever'."

The troops came to our shores not because of disorder but to *quell anticipated disorder* after our dismissal and the suspension of our Constitution.

The charges listed did not make out a case for our removal. What, then, are the reasons which prompted the Government to depose us? There are two main reasons.

First, if we had remained in office more than a few months the position of the Governor and the whole constitutional machinery would have been thoroughly exposed in the eyes of the people. Second, American pressure must obviously have been exerted on the British Government.

I will deal with these factors in the next chapter.

CHAPTER TEN

THE REAL CRISIS

"And since there are those who pretend to estimate the peoples,
Sum and divide them to suit the needs of their policy,
That for this class, this for that superior nation,
Shaped and assessed on the rate of their own order of merit,
These are some things I must say to them."

PETER BLACKMAN

The Governor's attitude towards our legislation was already exposing him by the time the British troops arrived in British Guiana.

The Upper House—the State Council—had already rejected two Bills that had been passed by the House of Assembly. One was the repeal of the Undesirable Publications Ordinance; the other was the repeal of the Rice Farmers' (Security of Tenure) Ordinance, 1945.

We were on the point of introducing other Bills.

There was the Reform of Local Government. As I have already indicated, this Bill sought to grant universal adult suffrage and to abolish nominated seats in the municipalities and village councils. On its introduction in the Executive Council, the Governor indicated to us that we should consult public opinion and take our proposals to the Village Chairmen's Conference and the Village Fathers.

We pointed out that these proposals had been part of our election manifesto, and the people had elected us on the basis of our programme. We also pointed out to him the reactionary nature of the Village Chairmen's Conference. However, in due deference to him we accepted his suggestion, took our proposals to the countryside and sought the view of the local authorities.

The Governor's move was, of course, a clever one. Our intention was to have the Bill passed before November 1953, in time for the local elections throughout the country. But the Governor hoped by his move to delay consideration of the Bill and also to generate enough opposition by the reactionaries in the local authorities to sustain him when he vetoed the Bill later. As he expected, these people indicated their disapproval of our proposals and were given wide publicity in the three capitalist newspapers.

The Labour Relations Bill, which I have already described, was passed on the day that troops landed in British Guiana.

Then we had the revised Land Law legislation, the purpose of which was to set up a Land Authority to tax uncultivated lands and examine the whole question of the beneficial use of these lands. There were the three taxes on the sugar planters—Excise, Acreage and Sugar Export duty. These would obviously have been rejected by the planters. And there were amendments to the laws granting tax and other concessions to foreign capital entering British Guiana in the mining industry.

Our Upper House was similar to the House of Lords. It could reject money Bills for three months and other Bills for one year. But our Constitution differed in one respect. If any major measure rejected by either of the two Houses was deemed by the Governor of vital importance to the economy of the country and the well-being of its inhabitants, then he could summon a joint meeting of both Houses before the necessary period of delay had elapsed.

We had intimated to the Governor that we wanted him to use his Constitutional power to summon a meeting of both Houses to consider particularly the Labour Relations Bill and the Local Government Bill. Had he refused, as no doubt he would, then we would have exposed him to the people.

If, on the other hand, he had summoned a joint meeting, then automatically the Bills would have gone to him to be signed. For we had a total of 20 out of 36 members—18 out of 27 in the Lower House and 2 out of 9 in the Upper House. But he need not, of course, have given his signature. His absolute veto would then have come into play.

In either case, therefore, the Governor would have become a very unpopular figure.

After the Governor's arrival in March 1953, he made frequent trips into the countryside with Lady Savage, trying to endear himself with the people by going into their shacks, cuddling farmers' babies and so on.

He told his hearers that the British Government was interested in their well-being, and as a servant of the Government he would do everything in his power to make their lives happier. But unfortunately he had not now the power; all power was in the hands of their elected Ministers! But he was prepared to support the elected Ministers so long as they continued to work on behalf of the people. Clearly, his opposition to our measures would have destroyed the veneer of popularity with which he had surrounded himself.

The people would also have understood why we had opposed the Constitution from its very inception. They would have understood why we were circulating to them a "Patriotic Appeal for Amendments to the Constitution".

The Government statement says the troops came to British Guiana to forestall a Communist plot on our part to destroy the Constitution and the administration of the colony; but they came really to forestall this imminent exposure of the Governor and the Constitution.

* * *

What about the second point—American pressure?

Immediately after our election, the American press became very conscious of events in British Guiana. *Time* magazine wrote of the first Communist Government being set up in the British Empire. Mr. Drew Pearson, a widely read American columnist, wrote a syndicated column warning the American people that while Americans were fighting to preserve democracy against Communism in far-off Korea, a Communist Government was being set up at their back door.

The American State Department also began to take a keen interest in the affairs of British Guiana.

The U.S. Vice-Consul, stationed in Trinidad, made repeated visits. About a month before we were removed from office, a Congressman, Mr. Jackson, visited our shores and was a guest of the Governor. On departing, Mr. Jackson remarked that British Guiana was within the strategic zone of the United States. This was in keeping with Professor Walter Rippey's contention that the Caribbean area was the danger zone of the U.S. During the war, the Americans built bases in Guiana and throughout the West Indies in exchange for some dilapidated destroyers.

What evidence is there of American interference in our affairs?

First, there is a statement by Mr. J. Campbell, chairman of Booker Bros., McConnell and Co., in London. On the first news of the despatch of troops, Mr. Campbell said that he did not see the reason for all the excitement and the necessity for troops, because so far as he was concerned the crisis was over. By the crisis he meant the five-week strike in the sugar estates which had been settled nearly two weeks earlier. This remark seems to indicate that while the planters were alarmed about our programme in relation to their vested interests, it was not mainly their pressure that forced the hand of the British Government.

The *Washington Post,* admitting that the election victory of the P.P.P. had caused some alarm in the United States, said it was necessary to deprive us of our limited rights and suggested the re-establishment of real authoritative power for the Governor.

The *New York Herald Tribune* said on October 9: "The British Guiana affair is of vital importance to the United States. Not because of the internal events within that colony but because of its strategic juxtaposition. Venezuela is the synonym for two very important items to the United States' economy—oil and iron ore."

The *Church Times* said on October 16: "Iron ore deposits covering 75 square miles have been discovered in Venezuela, near the British Guiana border. On the British Guiana side of the frontier iron ore deposits have also been discovered which may well be a continuation of those in Venezuela. They are claimed to be the biggest in the world.

"The frontier between British Guiana and Venezuela, moreover, in the region where the new iron ore deposits have been discovered, is in dispute. This is one reason for the American interest in the deterioration of the situation."

Many foreign companies, predominantly American, are now carrying out extensive exploratory investigations for manganese, oil and other strategic mineral deposits. Columbite-tantalite is now being mined by the Americans; it produces a high-heat-resisting metal (the only other source is Nigeria) useful for making jet bombers. A search is being made for radioactive thorium.

Americans have extensive interests in British Guiana. There is the Demerara Bauxite Co., with its sister company, Sprostons Ltd. Both these are subsidiaries of the Aluminium Co. of Canada, which is itself tied up to the giant monopoly, the Aluminium Co. of America, financed by Mellon, one of the biggest U.S. financiers. This company produced nearly 2½ million tons of bauxite in 1952.

The Berbice (Bauxite) Co. was recently bought by Reynolds Metals Co., another giant U.S. aluminium company. Other United States companies are the Kennecot Corporation and Harvey Aluminium Inc., which are now prospecting for bauxite.

No wonder the *Daily Mail* correspondent reported from Georgetown on October 9:

> "It is reported here reliably that the anxieties of the U.S. Government played a not inconsiderable part in Britain's decision to send troops to British Guiana. For the Americans have installations built during the war at the Atkinson airfield near here."

Naval and air bases were established during the war. The air base closed recently, but it can be re-occupied at any time.

Lyttelton's denial of any direct interference by the U.S. Government is too emphatic. During the House of Commons debate he said: "No representations of any kind were received from the U.S. Government before Her Majesty's Government made their decision."

This is the gentleman who on his return to London airport after the Queen had signed the Order-in-Council destroying our Constitution, said in reply to questions about the possibility of imminent Government action in Guiana: "Our journey to Balmoral was a normal visit from members of the Privy Council to the Queen."

The U.S. State Department was quick to bless the action of the British Government.

Mr. Henry Byroade, the U.S. Assistant Secretary of State for Near Eastern, South Asian and African Affairs, made a significant statement, soon after our Constitution was destroyed, about the rate at which colonial people must be given their freedom. *The Times* reported on November 2, 1953:

> "It is significant that it should have been an American spokesman who on Saturday felt compelled to issue a warning against the hasty shedding of their responsibilities by the Imperial powers . . . Mr. Henry Byroade, the Assistant Secretary of State for Near Eastern, S. Asian and African Affairs, while declaring that his country will use its influence to help colonial peoples towards self-government—thereby in most cases seconding the efforts to which the suzerain powers are pledged—adds a clear declaration of the perils of 'premature' independence."

Many Americans, however, take the view that the U.S. Government did not have anything to do with the rape of democracy in Guiana. At Patna, India, an American professor and his wife accosted me on this score. The view is still held by some that America today still cherishes the democratic beliefs of Jefferson, Paine, Patrick Henry, Lincoln and other American patriots, that there is no such thing as American imperialism. They point to the fact that America is prepared to give independence to Puerto Rico. They naively refer to America's interest in the development of backward areas and instance Point Four without perhaps realising the full significance of this so-called aid programme.

I am sorry to disillusion these people. The main aim of the Point Four programme is to prevent industrialisation of the so-called backward territories; to sell more U.S. equipment and pave the way for U.S. investments. This is admitted on all sides. The then Secretary of State, Dean Acheson, testifying before the Senate Foreign Relations Committee on the Point Four programme, said on March 30, 1950:

> "I think there is a pretty widely held idea that we are going to build large mills, mines and factories for these under-developed peoples. It is not true."

Mr. Eugene S. Gregg, vice-president of the Western Electric International, was even more open, according to the *New York Times* on May 5, 1952:

> "The Government's part in Point Four should be limited to such public spheres as health, education and port and transport development, particularly where the latter will bring quick increase of strategic raw materials needed by this country."

Commenting on Point Four, a special issue of the American fortnightly, *The Reporter,* more recently said: "We need the availability of raw materials without assuming the burden of conquering and ruling every country where they are to be found."

Yes, it is not necessary any longer to conquer. This involves too many headaches in administration. Just have a "friendly" government—as in Dutch Guiana which has a "nationalist" party in power and a Dutch army of occupation, but which is totally dependent on America (most of its revenue is derived from bauxite which goes to the U.S.).

Incidentally, this "nationalist" government dined and feted me during my brief visit a month before the suspension of our Constitution. But after our removal (no doubt taking instructions from America which refused even a transit visa for a passage through New York) it would not permit an overnight stay in Surinam to make plane connections.

This is the kind of friendly government the U.S. wants. If there should be "unfriendliness", then a pocket-army revolution, as in Latin America, is convenient. But where these revolutions are not customary, as in British Guiana, a few gunboats are useful.

These, then, were the main reasons for our dismissal. It was not our activities that "necessitated the movement of troops to preserve law and order". We were, as one writer puts it, "constitutional zealots". We were working the constitutional machinery provided while at the same time circulating for signatures a national petition, the "Patriotic Appeal for Amendments to the Constitution". We had no powers to amend the Constitution. All we could have done was to table the petition at the appropriate time in the House of Assembly, and later forward it to the Government in Britain.

Speaking of the "red plot", even our most bitter and consistent enemy, the editor of the *Daily Argosy*, a war-time security officer, knew "of no organised plan for such a revolt . . ." He said in an editorial on October 11:

> "What the P.P.P. leaders were aiming at (and all the evidence points that way) was a political and constitutional crisis, in the hope of going back to the country and returning with a renewed mandate that might with difficulty be questioned."

And this, of course, is a perfectly constitutional practice.

CHAPTER ELEVEN

DEMOCRACY ON TRIAL

"Tell your countrymen, when you return, what you have seen in England. Tell them the British Chartists are in the field; and scorning national antipathies, proclaim the brotherhood of man throughout the world—and are ready to prove their sincerity in your cause."

ERNEST JONES

There are those in the Labour Party who say that we had committed blunders and were going too fast. But perhaps it is time for some heart-searching and self-criticism on the part of our critics.

When the British Guiana crisis first arose, Mr. Morgan Phillips, secretary of the Labour Party, said at a meeting in Gloucester ; "If clear evidence of a plot is not forthcoming, the action which has been taken may call into question Britain's good faith towards development of self-government in the colonies".

Surely no clear evidence has been produced. Yet I am sorry to observe that the National Executive of the Labour Party in a statement of November 1953, while reaffirming "its belief in the promotion of democratic self-government in colonial territories", declared that it was "inadvisable for local Parties to provide a platform for P.P.P. speakers or to co-operate with other bodies (which might well be Communist-dominated) in supporting them".

This, of course, was most regrettable, especially as, I am told, the decision was taken by a majority of one. It emboldened Mr. Lyttelton, who soon after pounced on Buganda and deposed the Kabaka. In Guiana, five P.P.P. leaders, including the former Minister of Works and Communications, and two members of the House of Assembly, were detained. Two youth organisations and the Peace Committee were proscribed. The Governor banned a long list of publications, all of which could be bought in the streets of London.

This was the week when the British Government declared it was extending to all its 42 colonial territories the Convention of Human Rights, which it had ratified at the Council of Europe!

Fortunately the dictum of the National Executive was not accepted by the whole Labour movement. The Communist Party and the *Daily Worker,* the *Tribune* and other weeklies like *Forward, Socialist Outlook* and *Reynolds News* backed us fully.

Several prominent M.P.s, including the Bevanites, gave us strong support. Mr. Ian Mikardo, M.P., spoke on my platform in his constituency at Reading after the ban of the National Executive.

During our tour of Britain Mr. Burnham and I received enthusiastic rank-and-file support. Many individual members of the Labour Party—city councillors, Labour agents—defied the ban. Councillor Andrew Wood, chairing our large meeting in Glasgow, defiantly declared he still had "a lot of fight left in him".

Organisations such as the Union of Democratic Control, the Fabian Society and the League of Peoples Against Imperialism offered us a platform, and in a few places where the local people had become frightened, helped to arrange our meetings.

During our subsequent tour in India, Pakistan, Egypt and Europe, we found a tremendous reservoir of good will and support for our cause. Everywhere we noticed the keen interest taken in colonial affairs, and the resistance to what the Indian Prime Minister, Mr. Nehru, calls "the hardening of colonialism".

* * *

Two paths are open to the British Labour movement. One is to continue the exploitation of the colonial peoples ; the other is to work for the freedom and the liberation of colonial peoples.

The present British Government has chosen the first path. After destroying democracy in British Guiana it has now reduced government to a farce. In place of our democratically elected government, Mr. Lyttelton has substituted a nominated body made up of officials, former nominated members of the old Legislative Council and defeated candidates, five of whom lost their deposits at the 1953 elections. He has sent out a Constitution Commission to Guiana, not to write for us a better Constitution, but to revise the Constitution backwards. Note the terms of reference:

> "In the light of circumstances which make it necessary to suspend the Constitution of British Guiana, to consider and recommend what changes are required in it."

Not to enquire, of course, whether our actions necessitated the suspension of the Constitution.

There is no doubt about the outcome of the Commission's inquiry. Mr. Lyttelton has already said in the House of Commons that all the trouble in British Guiana would not have occurred if there had been an official majority in the Executive Council.

It is true that the British Government contemplates voting £3,125,000 from Colonial Development and Welfare as a grant for a five-year scheme of development involving a sum of £15 million. We welcome this. But it is like pouring water on a duck's back. The planters and their associates are now in the saddle. They will decide and administer. The money will go the way of other sums allocated in the past.

But what is more alarming is the new doctrine Mr. Lyttelton has pronounced. In the House of Commons on October 22, 1953, he said: "Her Majesty's Government is not prepared to tolerate the setting up of Communist states in the British Commonwealth".

The same thing was said in slightly different words and loudly cheered at the Conservative Party Conference in Margate on October 9. This is indeed something entirely new. It is a warning to the Labour movement in the Dominions, and, more particularly, in Britain. It is the language of Hitler. Be sure not to threaten the citadel of capitalism or troops will be used against you. Mr. Lyttelton uses the weapon of anti-Communism. So did Hitler.

But Mr. Lyttelton's definition of Communism is elastic. Anything which does not suit his imperialist interest can be deemed

Communist. We know what is happening in South Africa, where any criticism of the racialist apartheid policy of Malan's fascist Government is deemed Communist activity. In the Suppression of Communism Act, Communism is defined inter alia as : "Any doctrine or scheme (a) which aims at bringing about any political, industrial, social or economic change by the promotion of disturbances, or by unlawful acts and (b) which aims at the encouragement of feelings of hostility between the European and non-European races, calculated to further the objects mentioned at (a)."

The Rev. Michael Scott's booklet *Shadow over Africa* and the United Nations film *The People's Charter* were declared "subversive" and banned in South Africa.

Recently in British Guiana at my wife's trial for allegedly holding a public meeting against the Emergency Regulations, Mr. Nehru's autobiography *Towards Freedom* was declared by Government police officers a Communist book.

Mr. Aneurin Bevan, at a public meeting, challenged the Tory Government's action in British Guiana and Lyttelton's doctrine, which he interpreted as: "You are free to have whatever government you like as long as it is the kind of government we like."

The issue in Guiana today is not Communism. It is really whether any people—colonial people—have a right to rule themselves. This right, we are told, has been guaranteed to us by the Atlantic Charter which respected "the right of all people to choose the form of government under which they will live" and the United Nations Declaration of Human Rights, which recognised that "the will of the people shall be the basis of authority of government".

Neither the P.P.P. nor Communism is on trial. Democracy itself is on trial. Democracy, it is said, is based on ballots. But in our country, in the name of democracy, our elected Government was deposed by force and the threat of violence. The threat of bullets has replaced ballots.

Are the rights in the Atlantic Charter and the U.N. Declaration of Human Rights merely to be paper rights?

This is the challenge which all liberal-minded, democracy-loving people must accept. Guiana is the acid test. Western democracy will stand or fall to the extent that the Labour movement faces this challenge with its united strength.

Jennie Lee, M.P., at a crowded meeting in London cried: "A tidal wave of popular anger should sweep away the Tory Government because of its dictatorial policy in British Guiana."

The British Labour movement should rise to this call. It should return to the militancy of its good old days. It should speak out in strong language like the T.U.C. declaration of 1925 which said:

> "This Trades Union Congress believes that the domination of non-British peoples by the British Government is a form of capitalist exploitation having for its object the securing for British capitalists (1) of cheap sources of raw materials, (2) the right to exploit cheap and unorganised labour and to degrade workers' standards in Britain.
>
> "It declares its complete opposition to imperialism and resolves (1) to support all workers in all parts of the British Empire in organising trade unions and political parties in order to further their interests, and (2) to support the right of all peoples in the British Empire to self-determination, including the right to choose complete separation from the Empire."

The Labour movement must not let Mr. Lyttelton's red herring of Communism divide it; anti-Communism was the weapon used by Hitler to destroy the Labour movement. Divide and rule is the policy of capitalists and imperialists.

Lyttelton's policy is the path of exploitation, of looting and plunder of the colonial people and their resources. This, for the British people, has meant brutal and savage war as in Kenya and Malaya; it has meant conscription and less production, huge military expenditure, fewer subsidies and more hardship.

There is another path; the path of co-operation, understanding and equality for the mutual advantage of both colonial peoples and the people of Britain.

Let it be recorded by future historians that the British Labour movement played the decisive and progressive role at this critical juncture of Britain's and the world's history.

EPILOGUE

THE ROAD BACKWARD

"The British will write any constitution for a colony except a free constitution."

SYDNEY KING

The long-awaited Report of the Robertson Constitution Commission was tabled on November 2, 1954, in the House of Commons. It was simultaneously released in British Guiana and the West Indies. While Mr. Lennox-Boyd, Secretary of State for the Colonies, was addressing the Commons, Sir Alfred Savage was haranguing the Interim Leislative Council.

The Report has come as no surprise. Its recommendations were to me a foregone conclusion. Firstly, it completely justified and whitewashed the British Government's action in destroying our Constitution and removing my ministers and myself from office. In the words of the Commission: "We are satisfied that the set-back to orderly constitutional progress in British Guiana was due not to defects in the Constitution but to the fact that those in control of the People's Progressive Party proved themselves unscrupulous in their determination to pervert the authority of Government to their own disruptive and undemocratic ends."

"Disruptive and undemocratic ends" refers, needless to say, to the "sinister" extremists, the Communists. But while the red-herring of Communism has been given as the major reason for the rape of our Constitution, the burden of argument is that the Constitution was lost because of our previous attitude to it.

It is true that we were severely critical of the limitations of the Waddington Constitution—its Governor and nominated Upper House with delaying powers; its retention of the portfolios of finance, defence, foreign affairs, police, information and justice in the hands of Government officials appointed from London; and finally the veto and reserve powers of the Governor. But it is equally true that our views on the Constitution and for that matter on Communism were well known to

Whitehall before the elections and the assignment of our portfolios in April and May respectively of 1953.

The destruction of the Constitution was caused not by our refusal to work it because of preconceived views. The fact is we were working it. The snag came about because we were not working it according to the plans carefully laid down. The Constitutional structure was not designed to accommodate six P.P.P. ministers in a policy-making Executive Council of ten. But once having got control of the Executive Council our working of the Constitution could have led and was leading to only one inevitable conclusion—the exposure of the Governor and the limited Constitution. It was really to forestall this exposure that the troops marched in in October 1953, and not because of our "disruptive and undemocratic ends".

And what of the future? "We are, therefore, driven to the conclusion", said the Commission, "that so long as the P.P.P. retains its present leadership and policies there is no way in which any real measure of responsible government can be restored without the certainty that the country will again be subjected to constitutional crisis. . . . We can see no alternative but to recommend a period of marking time in the advance towards self-government."

The Waddington Commission did not have its nose to the ground. Assured that no party system would be fully developed in less than five to ten years, and assured that we would not win a majority at the General Elections, it dared to give us a "liberal" constitution with a policy-making executive council of 6 - 4 in favour of the elected Members. Our phenomenal success at the April 1953 elections of eighteen out of twenty-four seats clearly upset their time-table. That was their mistake.

The Robertson Commission, on the other hand, is not to be caught in the same trap. They have "sounded" the people. In this they have no doubt been helped by the advice of many spies and "impartial" observers who have visited our shores since October 9, 1953.

A London *Times* correspondent observed that we were "*deeply entrenched. . . . There is little doubt what the result of another general election would be. The P.P.P. remains the only organised political body in the sugar estates and the villages. The new Party, the National Democratic Party, has made little impact and is almost unknown in many places."*

Thus having found that the people's confidence is still 100 per cent behind the P.P.P., the Commission could come to only two conclusions. One, the proscription of the Party and the disenfranchisement of some of the "extremist" leaders. The other, postponement of the elections and "marking time".

The latter was accepted in preference to the former for two main reasons. Firstly, it is generally accepted that proscription does not really destroy. The Indian National Congress was banned, but it finally led the Indian people to political independence.

Secondly, disenfranchisement of the "extremist" leaders (however desirable from the commission's viewpoint) has its dangers. There is world public opinion to be reckoned with. It would have meant importing here the fascist methods of Dr. Malan of South Africa, whose government, after "naming" individuals as Communists, prohibits them from sitting in Parliament and holding official posts in trade unions.

But why the period of marking time? The Commission quite unashamedly considered "what the outcome would be of an immediate attempt to restore a measure of power to elected representatives, by which we mean a representative legislature and a retention of some form of ministerial system".

In paragraph 211, they said that we would more likely contest rather than boycott any elections and after such elections either.

(1) refuse to take our seats; or
(2) with a majority, refuse to elect ministers and thus be obstructive; or
(3) elect Ministers and again provoke a constitutional crisis.

The obvious answer to this is, so what! Isn't that strictly constitutional? Governor Savage has been persistently saying that all talk of non-co-operation is stupid. What is there left to the people? Are they to follow their masters and put guns in their hands?

Quite indefinite will be "this period of marking time", this period of stalemate and retrogression. The Commission lays it down: "We cannot estimate the length of the period which should elapse before the advance towards self-government is resumed. Everything will depend upon the extent to which the people of British Guiana, including the leaders of the P.P.P. themselves, can be brought to the realisation that the futile and deliberately disruptive policies for which the P.P.P. at present stands, are no basis for the future constitutional progress of this country."

In other words, the people must give up their present leaders. If they don't, there will be no hope of elections in the foreseeable future. But the Commission does not stop at this open threat. It goes on to suggest bribery, to encourage opportunism, splits and racial divisions, the old imperialist trick of divide and rule.

By "pump-priming" and quick social and economic improvements, the Commission wants the Government to win over the people from the "extremism" of the present leaders.

It is in this context that the present emphasis on housing must be viewed. But even here the Interim Government has shown its ineptitude.

Bitingly critical, one top C.D.C. (Colonial Development Corporation) official feels that the Government will hardly reach 10 per cent of its target for this and the following year. Past régimes have always excused themselves on the ground of shortage of lumber, properly seasoned and graded into standardised sizes. The new C.D.C. Sawmill at Houston was to be the panacea for all our housing ills.

There is no longer this old excuse. The new mill is not only up and producing but "overproducing". The C.D.C. can find no markets for more than 2 million board feet of lumber stacked up in its lumber yard. But more alarming is the disclosure that the company is not yet in possession of information on standardised sizes, for which repeated requests have been made during the past year. As a result, its second shift was closed down. More than 160 men were thrown out on the streets, swelling the number of the unemployed.

Recognising that no party has yet displaced or is likely to displace the P.P.P. in the foreseeable future, the Commission sees as the only way out for imperialism a split in the ranks of the P.P.P. along ideological and racial lines. It divides the leadership into "extremist" Communists and "democratic" socialists, and suggests that the latter, around whom the people should rally, should split from the former.

On page 70, I alluded to the expulsion in 1952 of the so-called Reds, Richard Hart, Arthur Henry, Ken Hill and Frank Hill from the People's National Party (P.N.P.) of Jamaica. What I omitted, but what should be fully emphasised here, is the resultant weakening of the anti-imperialist, anti-Bustamante forces. In place of a united single party (P.N.P.) and single trade union front (T.U.C.), there are now three separate trade union and political groupings opposed to Bustamante's forces. This is what the Commission wants for Guiana.

And then it seeks to sow the seeds of racial dissension by attacking the Indians, the majority racial group. The Indian element, it says, has now shaken off its previous lethargy. It raises the old bogey of Indian educational and commercial success being a threat to the security of the other races, particularly the Africans who constitute the second major race group. "Their very success", it asserts, "in these spheres has begun to awaken the fears of the African section of the population, and it cannot be denied that since India received her independence in 1947 there has been a marked self-assertiveness amongst Indians in British Guiana. Guianese of African extraction were not afraid to tell us that many Indians in British Guiana looked forward to the day when British Guiana would be a part not of the British Commonwealth but of an East Indian Empire. The result has been a tendency for racial tension to increase . . . today the relationships are strained; they present an outward appearance which masks the feelings of suspicion and distrust."

Mr. C. R. Jacob, President of the East Indian Association, roundly attacked this viewpoint which he described as "purely fictitious". He went on to state: "There is greater unity today than there ever was in the history of this country, and it is because of this unity that Guianese witnessed the great conspiracy of last year which resulted in the rape of the Waddington Constitution".

The Commission has lastly dangled the "golden apple" of a

new constitution, just in case the path of betrayal and treachery so meticulously laid down be chosen by the people. It is more illiberal than, and a slight variation of, the Waddington Constitution. The Executive Council of the future should be a balance of five elected and five official plus nominated members, with the Governor as President holding a casting vote. This bears out my predictions as set out on page 94: "There is no doubt about the outcome of the Commission's inquiry. Mr. Lyttelton has already said in the House of Commons that all the trouble in British Guiana would not have occurred if there had been an official majority in the Executive Council."

As a side-track, the Commission recommended the appointment of a Commissioner who will completely overhaul the local government set-up. I have already set out on pages 75 and 85 the undemocratic local government structure, and the reforms we proposed. It is hardly expected that adult suffrage and abolition of nominated seats will materialise under the present dictatorial government. Nor will any real changes be made in the composition and autocratic powers of the Local Government Board.

In the interim, there will be no local government elections. Municipal elections for Georgetown and New Amsterdam due next month are indefinitely postponed. As I write a draft bill has appeared in the Official Gazette. No doubt it is an indication of forthcoming events.

The Governor is to be given even more powers than he has at the moment. If the seat of an elected member becomes vacant because of death, resignation or passage of time, there will be no election or bye-election. The Governor will nominate a member. If there is a tie in the selection of the Mayor by the Councillors, the Governor will select one from among the Councillors. Under the Town Council Ordinance, in case of a tie the ultimate choice is the voters'.

Boiled down to its barest essentials, the Robertson Commission's dictum is this—You can vote, but you mustn't vote for the people who are going to fight for you.

This interpretation of democracy is in keeping with Lyttelton's action of October 9, 1953. Mr. A. Lennox-Boyd, the new

Secretary of State for the Colonies, concurs with this view. The only difference is that while he agrees with the Commission that there should be no limits to "the period of marking time", he has specifically set December 1957 as the life of the present nominated Legislature Council with its six defeated candidates (five of whom lost their deposits).

Everyone, however, is not in agreement with this view. The *Manchester Guardian* warned: *"The one thing that cannot be accepted is to let Guiana stagnate as it has stagnated for too many of the last fifty years and to cover the lack of progress by a fixed and immovable bureaucracy. Better than that, put Jagan back in power and let him do his best or his worst."*

"Stagnate", however is not the correct word. It is not precise enough. For what we have is not "stagnation" but "retrogression". During the past year, we have not been standing still; we have been going backwards.

The "immovable" bureaucracy has trampled even the limited rights we enjoyed. For nearly six months, I saw the inside of a jail for violating an order made by the Governor restricting my movements within the Georgetown area. Actually at the time of my arrest, I was attending to my patients at the branch surgery about thirty-five miles from Georgetown.

Here is a list of some of the others who have graced H.M.'s jail for allegedly committing offences—actually for exercising rights guaranteed under the Universal Declaration of Human Rights and the Convention on Human Rights ratified by the British Government:

For being in possession of "subversive", banned literature—Dr. J. P. Lachmansingh (former Minister of Health and Housing), Mohamed Khan and Fred Bowman (former members of the House of Assembly).

For demonstrating and holding meetings—Nasrudeen, Salim, Ajodha Singh, S. Lachmansingh, Martin Carter, Eric Huntley, Rory Westmaas, Pandit Misir, Eustace Sam, Larry Duncan, Edwin Mercurius, Eric Brathwaite, Mildred Ramoudit, Hoosein, Cecil Sampson, Richard Verbeke.

For failure to report daily to police—Fred Bowman, Ram Karran and Rory Westmaas.

P.P.P.s General Secretary, Janet Jagan, is now serving four three-month sentences for holding a meeting, demonstrating, and being in possession of banned literature and a copy of *Police Riot Drill Manual.* Others have been jailed and fined for simply shouting "P.P.P. for ever", "Long live the P.P.P."

Last year almost immediately after British troops landed, five, including the Minister of Communications and Works, Mr. Sydney King, and two members of the House of Assembly, were detained. At the moment eight are languishing at a concentration camp in the interior, Mazaruni Settlement.

Another caustic critic of the Commission's recommendations is Mr. Richard Crossman, Labour M.P. Writing in the *Sunday Pictorial* he said that before giving Russia any more lectures on her alleged refusal to permit free elections in East Germany, Britain should look at two of her colonies—Cyprus and British Guiana. "The moral is obvious", he commented.

Now that the mask is definitely off the British Government's nauseating hypocrisy about "advancing the peoples in the colonial territories to the goal of democratic self-government as their political development and economic stability will allow", it is for the Labour movement in Britain to state clearly its position. Does it support the narrow strictures *et al* on democracy? Or does it hold on to the old tenets of democracy—government of the people, for the people and by the people?

As colonials, we are most anxiously looking on. The people of Guiana may mark time, but certainly not to the time of imperialism. I for one do not intend to play the role of stooge colonial leader such as Britain loves to parade before the world. I will not rest until my country is free.

CHEDDI JAGAN,

Georgetown, B.G.,

November 26, 1954.